MW01245044

THE BLESSED HOPE OF THE CHURCH

THE RAPTURE

DON STEWART

The Rapture:
An Introduction To The Blessed Hope Of The Church

By Don Stewart

© 2016 Don Stewart

Revised and updated in 2014 from a larger work written in 2002. This earlier work can now be found on my CD "Don Stewart's Answers To Over 1,600 Bible Questions Christians Often Ask" (Originally published by the Net Bible Institute (2002) and The Bible Explorer Website (2007).

Published By ETW (Educating The World) San Dimas, California
All rights reserved

VERSES ARE CITED FROM THE HOLY BIBLE, NEW INTERNATIONAL VERSION, COPYRIGHT 2011 BY INTERNATIONAL BIBLE SOCIETY. ALL RIGHTS RESERVED

TABLE OF CONTENTS

INTRODUCTION

In this book we will take an introductory look at one of the major issues on the subject of Bible prophecy popularly known as the "rapture" of the church. The term rapture refers to the "catching away" of living believers to meet Jesus Christ. This happens at the same time as the resurrection from the dead of those who have died "in Christ."

While many Christians know certain things about this important doctrine there is still much ignorance about the subject. Indeed, too few Bible-believers can explain what they believe about this coming event let alone correctly give details of other views. This book attempts to clear up this lack of knowledge.

OUR GOAL

The goal of our book is to *accurately* present each major position with respect to the fact of the rapture as well as to its timing. We will do this in such a way that everyone understands exactly what various Bible-believers are saying as well as *why* they are saying it. We will do our best to list their strengths and weaknesses and then come to a conclusion as to which theory we feel best fits the facts.

As stated, this is an introductory work on the subject; it is not meant to be exhaustive. Consequently, we have chosen the main arguments which are usually brought up to support each position. We are well-aware that other things can be said to support the various theories. This is beyond the scope of what we are trying to accomplish in this introductory volume.

This Is The First Of Two Volumes On The Subject

In addition, there are other issues regarding the rapture of the church that space does not permit us to deal with in this introductory work. Consequently, we have planned a companion volume which will provide in-depth answers to some of the other often-asked questions on this subject. This will include some of the more technical issues.

OUR VIEWPOINT ON THE TIMING OF THE RAPTURE

At the outset it is important to let the reader know our perspective on this subject. It is our opinion that when all the evidence is considered the Pre-Tribulation view best lines up with the biblical facts. Simply stated, believers in Jesus Christ will be taken out of the world seven years before the Second Coming of Christ to the earth and will therefore escape the terrible time which the people on earth will experience known as the "time of Jacob's trouble," the "great tribulation" or the "seventieth week of Daniel." As you read the book you will discover why we come to this decision.

However, it is also recognized that many godly Bible-believers disagree with this conclusion. We understand this and have no problem with it. Indeed, since we are dealing with predictions of future events it is necessary to hold our viewpoint with charity and graciousness toward others. So if we do disagree on this issue, we should do it agreeably. This is the attitude which honors Christ.

With this in mind let us now look at the fascinating subject of the rapture of the church.

QUESTION 1

What Is The Rapture Of The Church?

One of the major prophetic events that the Bible speaks of is known as the "rapture of the church." It is also referred to as the "translation of the church." What is the rapture? What does the Bible tell us about this coming event?

The doctrine of the rapture of the church can be simply stated as follows. At some future time, the *genuine* believers in Jesus Christ (not merely people who have a church membership or affiliation) will be caught up to meet Him in the air when He descends from heaven. Those Christians who are alive will be instantaneously changed from their mortal bodies into immortal bodies, from corruptible bodies to incorruptible bodies. Immediately before this happens, the believers who have died "in Christ" will be raised from the graves into their new bodies where they too will be with the Lord. This is the "blessed hope" of the true believers in Jesus.

UNDERSTANDING THE TERMS RAPTURE, TRANSLATION, AND SECOND COMING

It is important that we understand the different terms used for the coming of the Lord; rapture, translation, and Second Coming. The terms rapture and translation are used for the coming of Jesus Christ *for* His church. In this coming, Jesus meets the believers *in the air*. The term Second Coming is consistently used as a reference to Jesus' coming back *to the earth* with the believers to establish His kingdom.

While the words rapture and translation refer to the same event they are not identical. The rapture refers to the doctrine that the believers in Christ are "caught up" from the earth to meet the Lord in the air. The term translation emphasizes that those who are snatched up are immediately transformed. The physical bodies of those who are raptured are instantly changed from natural, corruptible, mortal bodies to spiritual, incorruptible, immortal bodies. For simplicity sake, we will use the two terms, rapture and translation, interchangeably.

WHERE DO WE GET THE TERM RAPTURE?

The English term rapture is derived from the Latin Vulgate translation of the New Testament. The Latin verb *rapere* is a translation of the Greek word *harpadzo* which has the meaning of being "caught up." It is the word used in one of main passages describing this event, 1 Thessalonians 4:17. The believers are "caught up" to be with the Lord (Greek *harpadzo*, Latin *rapere*). Hence, the English word "rapture" comes to us by way of the Greek and the Latin.

We should note that while *rapere* is a verb meaning "to catch away" this catching away of believers has been turned into a noun, "the rapture." Thus, "the rapture" has become the popular way to portray this predicted catching away of believers.

We can make the following general observations about the doctrine of the rapture of the church.

1. THE BELIEVERS WILL BE CAUGHT UP

The Scripture speaks of this great catching away of the true believers in Jesus Christ. The Apostle Paul wrote to the church at Corinth and stated it in this manner.

> I declare to you, brothers and sisters, that flesh and blood cannot inherit the kingdom of God, nor does the perishable inherit the imperishable. Listen, I tell you a mystery: We will not all sleep, but we will all be changed-- in a flash, in the twinkling of an eye, at the last trumpet. For the trumpet will sound, the dead will be raised imperishable, and we will be changed (1 Corinthians 15:50-52).

When Paul speaks of "sleep" in this context he is referring to physical death. Not everyone will die! Millions of believers in Jesus Christ will be changed in the twinkling of an eye. This change will involve receiving a new body which is immortal and incorruptible. Those who have died in Christ will be raised with their new incorruptible bodies.

Paul told the church at Thessalonica something similar. He wrote to them of a time when the Lord Jesus would personally return for the believers and snatch them away to meet Him in the air.

He put it this way.

> For the Lord himself will come down from heaven, with a loud command, with the voice of the archangel and with the trumpet call of God, and the dead in Christ will rise first. After that, we who are still alive and are left will be caught up together with them in the clouds to meet the Lord in the air. And so we will be with the Lord forever (1 Thessalonians 4:16-17)

This passage emphasizes that the dead in Christ will rise first and then the living believers will be caught up to meet the Lord in the air.

2. JESUS SPOKE OF COMING FOR HIS OWN

Another passage which speaks of this event comes from the words of the Lord Jesus Himself. On the night of His betrayal, Christ told His disciples that He would come back for them. John records Him saying.

Do not let your hearts be troubled. You believe in God; believe also in me. My Father's house has many rooms; if that were not so, would I have told you that I am going there to prepare a place for you? And if I go and prepare a place for you, I will come back and take you to be with me that you also may be where I am (John 14:1-3).

These verses speak of Jesus "coming again" to take the believers to Himself, the rapture.

3. IT IS THE BLESSED HOPE OF BELIEVERS

When the Apostle Paul wrote to Titus he spoke of this event as the "blessed hope" of the church. He put it this way.

For the grace of God has appeared that offers salvation to all people. It teaches us to say "No" to ungodliness and worldly passions, and to live self-controlled, upright and godly lives in this present age, while we wait for the blessed hope--the appearing of the glory of our great God and Savior, Jesus Christ, who gave himself for us to redeem us from all wickedness and to purify for himself a people that are his very own, eager to do what is good (Titus 2:11-14)

While believers are presently fighting a spiritual battle in this world we are waiting for that "blessed hope;" the time Jesus Christ comes back for all of us.

In the same manner Paul wrote to the Philippians of this hope. He stated it in this manner.

But our citizenship is in heaven. And we eagerly await a Savior from there, the Lord Jesus Christ who, by the power that enables him to bring everything under his control, will transform our lowly bodies so that they will be like his glorious body (Philippians 3:20-21).

This is the hope of the believer. Our frail sinful bodies will be transformed by Jesus at the time of the rapture.

4. ENOCH AND ELIJAH ILLUSTRATE THE RAPTURE

The rapture of the church, the "catching away" of living believers who will not experience death, is not without a biblical precedent. Indeed, there are two Old Testament examples of people who did not suffer physical death; Enoch and Elijah. We read the following about Enoch.

> Enoch walked faithfully with God; then he was no more, because God took him away (Genesis 5:24).

God "took" Enoch to Himself. This faithful man of God did not have to experience physical death. The New Testament uses Enoch as an example of the rapture of the church. We read in Hebrews.

> By faith Enoch was taken from this life, so that he did not experience death: "He could not be found, because God had taken him away." For before he was taken, he was commended as one who pleased God (Hebrews 11:5).

The general rule is that every human being will die. The Bible makes this clear.

> Just as people are destined to die once, and after that to face judgment (Hebrews 9:27).

Enoch was an exception. He was "caught up" to meet the Lord.

Like Enoch, the prophet Elijah did not experience death. The Bible explains it this way.

> As they were walking along and talking together, suddenly a chariot of fire and horses of fire appeared and separated the two of them, and Elijah went up to heaven in a whirlwind (2 Kings 2:11).

Elijah was taken up in a whirlwind to meet the Lord while he was still alive.

As Enoch and Elijah did not suffer physical death, at some unknown time in the future, there will be millions of Christians who will have the same experience.

5. JESUS' ASCENSION INTO HEAVEN IS SOMETIMES USED AS AN ILLUSTRATION OF THE RAPTURE

Another event which is compared to the rapture of the church is the ascension of Jesus into heaven. The Bible describes it this way.

> After he said this, he was taken up before their very eyes, and a cloud hid him from their sight. They were looking intently up into the sky as he was going, when suddenly two men dressed in white stood beside them. "Men of Galilee," they said, "why do you stand here looking into the sky? This same Jesus, who has been taken from you into heaven, will come back in the same way you have seen him go into heaven" (Acts 1:9-11).

This is sometimes used as another illustration of what will occur to believers at the rapture of the church. However, there are differences. For one thing, Jesus' ascension took place *after* His death. Yet the catching up of living believers upon the earth will occur *before* they have died. Also, Jesus' ascension was in full view of His disciples while the gathering up of believers will seemingly not be seen by those remaining upon the earth. The Christians will simply disappear with nothing "left behind."

This briefly sums up the doctrine of the rapture of the church; the catching up of living believers into the presence of the Lord as well as the dead in Christ being simultaneously raised to meet Him. At that time both the dead and the living will be clothed with incorruptible immortal bodies. What a wonderful event this will be! Indeed, it is the "blessed hope" of the Christian.

SUMMARY TO QUESTION 1
WHAT IS THE RAPTURE OF THE CHURCH?

The rapture of the church is a term that is commonly used of the "catching up" of the church, the genuine believers in Jesus Christ, to meet their Lord in the air. At some point in the future, those Christians who are alive will have their mortal bodies transformed into incorruptible, immortal bodies. Immediately before this happens, the believers who have died will be raised from the dead and will also receive a new body as they meet Christ in the air. According to Scripture all of this will occur in a moment, in a twinkling, or in a blink, of an eye.

The rapture is distinct from the Second Coming in that it refers to the believers on earth being caught up to meet the Lord in the air and then return to heaven. The Second Coming is the return of Christ from heaven to the earth. While the rapture is often called the "translation" of the church the two words have a slightly different meaning. The rapture is the actual "catching up" of believers while the translation is the change which occurs to these believers. Their mortal physical corruptible bodies are changed into immortal, spiritual incorruptible bodies.

There are two passages in the writings of the Apostle Paul which directly speak of the rapture of the church; 1 Thessalonians 4:13-18 and 1 Corinthians 15:50-52. John 14:1-3 records Jesus promising to come back for His own. On the night of His betrayal, John records that Jesus told His disciples that He would come again for those who are "His" and bring them to Himself. This is the first biblical statement about the rapture, or translation, of true believers. In writing to Titus, the Apostle Paul speaks of this coming of Christ for His own as our "blessed hope."

This future event is not without precedent. There have been two previous biblical examples of this type of episode occurring. The first was the patriarch Enoch. The Book of Genesis tells us that the Lord simply took him away. He did not experience physical death. The second example is that of Elijah the prophet. The Bible says that he was taken to heaven in a whirlwind. He, like Enoch did not experience physical death. Therefore, we have a biblical model for this coming event known as the translation of the church, or the rapture of the church, where living believers will not have to die before they meet the Lord.

The ascension of Jesus into heaven is sometimes used as an illustration of the rapture. However, in Jesus' case this was His ascension *after* His resurrection from the dead. In the case of living believers, those who are translated or raptured will not experience physical death. Furthermore, Jesus' ascension was in full view of the apostles while it seems like the rapture will cause living believers to simply disappear from sight. Nobody will see them ascending into heaven and there will be no trace of these believers left on the earth.

This sums up what the Scripture teaches about this glorious event. The dead shall be raised in new bodies to meet Jesus Christ while the living believers will be instantly brought into His presence. Those who are alive will also be given new bodies which are immortal and incorruptible. This is indeed the "blessed hope" for the believer.

QUESTION 2

Why Should The Subject Of
The Rapture Be Studied?

Before we begin our study of the rapture of the church it is necessary to explain why we should take the time to examine this particular subject. Aren't there more important things to spend our time with than studying about the rapture? Indeed, what does this particular topic have to do with the way in which we conduct our daily lives?

While there are those that believe the subject of the rapture of the church is irrelevant, or should be limited to theologians who like to endlessly argue such issues, this is certainly not the case.

We can make a number of observations as to why this subject should be studied by everyone.

1. ALL SCRIPTURE IS PROFITABLE FOR STUDY

The first point we must make is that *all* Scripture is "profitable" or "useful" for us. The Apostle Paul wrote the following words to Timothy emphasizing this fact.

> All Scripture is God-breathed and is useful for teaching, rebuking, correcting and training in righteousness, so that the servant of God may be thoroughly equipped for every good work (2 Timothy 3:16-17)

"All" Scripture includes the topic of the rapture of the church. Since the teaching on the subject of the rapture is part of Holy Scripture, and all Scripture is useful, then this doctrine should be studied seeing that it will be beneficial to us.

2. WE SHOULD ATTEMPT TO UNDERSTAND THE PLAN OF GOD

When Paul met with elders from the church in Ephesus he commanded them to teach "the whole will, or plan, of God." The Bible records him saying.

> Therefore, I declare to you today that I am innocent of the blood of any of you. For I have not hesitated to proclaim to you the whole will of God (Acts 20:26-27).

Since the topic of the rapture of the church is part of God's overall plan for the human race it is crucial that we have some understanding of it.

3. THE APOSTLE PAUL MADE THIS SUBJECT A PRIORITY IN HIS TEACHING

The Apostle Paul was in Thessalonica for less than a month. However, during that time, he taught them on the subject of the "rapture of the church."

After writing to them about the final Antichrist, the coming Temple, and the rapture, he stated the following.

> Don't you remember that when I was with you I used to tell you these things? (2 Thessalonians 2:5)

If the Apostle Paul thought it was important enough to teach this subject in the short time that he was with these believers then we too should have the same attitude towards this topic. It is important!

4. WE WILL KNOW WHAT IS GOING TO TAKE PLACE IN THE FUTURE

Everyone wants to know what is going to happen in the future. When we study the subject of the rapture we will have a clearer picture as to what Scripture says will actually take place. In other words, we will be intelligently informed about coming events as predicted in the Bible.

5. THERE ARE PRACTICAL REASONS AS TO WHY

In addition to all of these points, there are also a number of practical reasons as to why this doctrine is important for us to study. Indeed, the position we hold concerning the timing of the rapture will determine the way in which we conduct our daily lives. In other words, we will have to make some decisions based upon our view of the timing of the rapture.

HOW SHALL WE LIVE?

Should we expect the return of Jesus Christ for the believers at any moment? Or should we expect to endure years of terrible events before Christ comes back? If so, then how should we prepare ourselves for this coming "great tribulation?"

If we believe the rapture can occur at "any moment" then we will live in expectancy of that event. However, if a number of events must take place before the rapture occurs then we will be looking for those things to happen. Indeed, we will *not* be looking for the immediate return of our Lord.

So, as we see, our understanding of the timing of the rapture of the church has enormous implications as to how we will conduct our lives and prepare for the future.

To sum up, we acknowledge that the subject of the rapture is not the most important issue which a person can examine. But neither is it irrelevant. In fact, there are a number of excellent reasons as to why we should take the time to look at this very relevant subject. This is what this book attempts to do.

SUMMARY TO QUESTION 2
WHY SHOULD THE SUBJECT OF THE RAPTURE BE STUDIED?

There are a number of reasons as to why we should engage in studying about the rapture.

First, it is part of Scripture. Since all Scripture is useful or profitable for us we should make this a part of our study.

God has given us the outline of His plan for time and eternity. The rapture of the church is part of that plan. Therefore, it is worth our time and effort to investigate what He has said.

We find that the Apostle Paul made this subject a priority in his teaching. Since he thought this to be an important subject to address then so should we.

Moreover, this particular study can give us assurance about our own future. We can know what is going to take place because the Bible tells us.

Finally, there are a number of practical reasons as to why this subject is important. Indeed, if we believe that we are meant to go through the great tribulation period, or some part of it, then we must prepare for that eventuality. However, if we believe that Christ can come back at any moment then we will live our lives with that truth always in our mind. In addition, we should also have a certain urgency about spreading the Word of God to the lost for Christ could return for us at "any moment."

As can be seen, there are numerous reasons as to why we should take the time to study the subject of the rapture of the church.

QUESTION 3

What Specific Truths Do We Learn About The Rapture From Scripture?

There are three main passages which specifically teach the doctrine of the rapture of the church (John 14:1-3, 1 Thessalonians 4:13-18 and 1 Corinthians 15:50-58). While other passages possibly speak of this coming event, these passages provide direct references to it.

When we put these passages together and compare what they teach, there are a number of specific things we can conclude about this event as well as its meaning for us. In fact, there are at least fourteen things which we learn about the rapture of the church from a study of these verses. They can be listed as follows.

1. THE LORD DOES NOT WANT US TO BE UNINFORMED OF THESE TRUTHS ABOUT THE RAPTURE

With respect to the rapture of the church, first and foremost we find that the Lord wants us to know certain things about this important truth. Paul wrote to the Thessalonians.

> Brothers and sisters, we do not want you to be uninformed about those who sleep in death, so that you do not grieve like the rest, who have no hope (1 Thessalonians 4:13).

This is essential for us to understand. Paul made the point that he did not want the Thessalonians to be uninformed of this truth. This assumes that they were ignorant but it also assumes they *could know* certain things about this coming event. Like the Thessalonians, we should not be uninformed of the truths regarding the rapture.

In the immediate context, Paul did not want them to be uninformed about the fate of believers which had died. He would now instruct them as to what had happened to these people. The Thessalonians would learn that these deceased believers were not at a disadvantaged because of their death.

In doing so, Paul emphasized that their grief over the loss of loved ones is different from the grief of unbelievers. The non-Christians have no hope. Those who have died believing in Jesus Christ have hope! We are allowed to experience sorrow but we should not be sorrowful like those which have no genuine hope for the future.

2. THIS TRUTH OF THE RAPTURE IS GIVEN BY THE WORD OF THE LORD

Next we find Paul saying that the doctrine of the rapture of the church was something he taught them "by the Word of the Lord." He wrote.

> According to the Lord's word, we tell you that we who are still alive, who are left till the coming of the Lord, will certainly not precede those who have fallen asleep (1 Thessalonians 4:15).

This stresses the divine authority of this doctrine. The fact that Paul emphasized that this teaching comes from "the Word of the Lord" gives further importance to that which he wrote.

Exactly what it meant by the phrase "the Word of the Lord" is not known. There have been a number of suggestions.

JESUS' TEACHINGS IN THE OLIVET DISCOURSE

There are those who believe Paul is referring to the Olivet Discourse of Jesus as recorded in Matthew 24-25. However, this is highly debatable.

We find nothing little, or nothing, specific in the Olivet Discourse which teaches these truths that Paul is speaking of here.

A TEACHING OF JESUS NOT RECORDED IN THE NEW TESTAMENT

Some argue that this doctrine was taught by Jesus in more detail but, for some reason, His words were not recorded in the New Testament. However, this does not seem likely given the fact that Paul states that he was the one to whom this truth was first fully revealed rather than to Jesus' Twelve disciples.

THIS WAS A DIRECT REVELATION GIVEN TO PAUL

More likely is the idea that Paul received this truth by direct revelation. In other words, the exact details were basically unknown to the believers until the time God revealed them to Paul.

Whatever the case may be, the doctrine of the rapture is God's truth. This is stressed by the apostle.

3. JESUS HAS PROMISED TO RETURN FOR HIS OWN

The rapture doctrine provides further details concerning the promise of Jesus to His disciples. From the words of Jesus on the night of His betrayal, we find the promise of His return. The Lord said that He will bring those who belong to Him, the Christians, back to Himself. John records Jesus saying the following.

> My Father's house has plenty of room; if that were not so, would I have told you that I am going there to prepare a place for you? And if I go and prepare a place for you, I will come back and take you to be with me that you also may be where I am (John 14:2-3).

Though Jesus said that He was going to go away from them, He also said a place was being prepared for these disciples. Thus, Jesus promised to return someday for those who are His. At His return, Jesus would then take these believers to be with Him in His Father's house.

However, the specific details of that return were not given by Jesus at that time. This would be the job of the Apostle Paul.

4. THIS IS A MYSTERY OR SACRED SECRET WHICH WAS NEVER BEFORE REVEALED

We also learn that this doctrine of the rapture of the church was first revealed to the Apostle Paul. He wrote.

> Listen, I tell you a mystery: We will not all sleep, but we will all be changed (1 Corinthians 15:51).

The doctrine of the rapture is a "mystery." This does not mean something which is difficult to comprehend. Instead the word has the idea of a "sacred secret." There was no divine revelation of this truth to the people of God before Paul unveiled it. He had written about it previously to the Thessalonians and now he is further explaining it to the Corinthians.

Consequently, since these truths were given to Paul to reveal, we should not look for the rapture doctrine in the Old Testament or, for that matter, even highlighted in the teachings of Jesus. While Jesus spoke of coming again for His own He did not elaborate on the details. This responsibility was given to the Apostle Paul.

Now let us look at the details of the event itself.

5. THE LORD HIMSELF WILL DESCEND FROM HEAVEN

The first thing we learn concerning this event, the rapture of the church, is that the Lord Jesus Himself will leave heaven to gather His own unto Himself. In other words, He initiates it. We read.

> For the Lord himself will come down from heaven, with a loud command, with the voice of the archangel and with the trumpet call of God, and the dead in Christ will rise first (1 Thessalonians 4:16).

The Lord will descend from heaven to commence this event. The fact that Jesus will leave heaven's glory speaks of something which is going to be very special.

6. THERE WILL BE A SHOUT OR A LOUD COMMAND FROM JESUS WITH THE VOICE OF AN ARCHANGEL

Paul also wrote that the voice of Jesus will be heard. He put it this way.

> For the Lord himself will come down from heaven, with a loud command, with the voice of the archangel and with the trumpet call of God, and the dead in Christ will rise first (1 Thessalonians 4:16).

There are a couple of things to note about this. First, we are told that Jesus will leave heaven with a shout or a "loud command." Interestingly, there are two instances during Jesus' earthly ministry where it is recorded that His shouting had an effect on the dead.

AT THE TOMB OF LAZARUS

At the tomb of Lazarus, who had been dead for four days, we read the following.

> When he had said this, Jesus called in a loud voice, "Lazarus, come out!" (John 11:43).

In this case, Lazarus came back from the dead after Jesus called out to him with a loud voice.

HIS LAST WORDS ON THE CROSS

We also find Jesus shouting or crying out His last words on the cross. In this instance, Matthew tells us that the graves of some of the righteous dead were opened and they came forth.

> And when Jesus had cried out again in a loud voice, he gave up his spirit. At that moment the curtain of the temple was

torn in two from top to bottom. The earth shook, the rocks split and the tombs broke open. The bodies of many holy people who had died were raised to life. They came out of the tombs after Jesus' resurrection and went into the holy city and appeared to many people (Matthew 27:50-53).

At the rapture of the church Jesus will give a shout, or cry of command, and again we will find that this affects those who are dead.

HIS VOICE WILL BE LIKE AN ARCHANGEL

Second, we are specifically told that His voice will be like that of an archangel. This is not the voice *of* an archangel, as some have supposed, but a voice *like* that of an archangel. In other words, it is a powerful voice.

7. THE TRUMPET OF GOD SHALL SOUND

We are also informed that the trumpet of God shall sound when the Lord descends from heaven. Paul wrote.

> For the Lord himself will come down from heaven, with a loud command, with the voice of the archangel and with the trumpet call of God, and the dead in Christ will rise first (1 Thessalonians 4:16).

Trumpets are used in Scripture to signify important occasions. The trumpet blast is certainly appropriate here as the Lord Himself will descend from heaven to bring the believers, living and dead, to Himself. As to who will actually hear this trumpet blast we are not told.

8. THOSE WHO HAVE DIED IN CHRIST WILL BE RAISED WITH NEW BODIES

The sequence continues. This rapture event will first involve the resurrection of the bodies of the believing dead "in Christ." Paul wrote about this to the Thessalonians.

For the Lord himself will come down from heaven, with a loud command, with the voice of the archangel and with the trumpet call of God, and the dead in Christ will rise first (1 Thessalonians 4:16).

These dead are presently in the presence of the Lord as perfect or perfected spirits. Yet they have *not* received their glorified body. At this future time, their perfect spirits will be joined with a perfect body. While they may have a temporary body they still await their future body. This will occur at the time of the rapture of the church.

These dead "in Christ" will be raised in incorruptible, immortal bodies. Paul wrote about this to the Corinthians putting it this way.

I declare to you, brothers and sisters, that flesh and blood cannot inherit the kingdom of God, nor does the perishable inherit the imperishable. Listen, I tell you a mystery: We will not all sleep, but we will all be changed-- in a flash, in the twinkling of an eye, at the last trumpet. For the trumpet will sound, the dead will be raised imperishable, and we will be changed (1 Corinthians 15:50-52).

Thus, the order of events involves the dead believers rising first. They will not miss out on this glorious event of the Lord's coming.

9. THE LIVING BELIEVERS WILL BE CAUGHT UP TO MEET THE LORD IN THE AIR

Those who are alive at that time, and who have believed in Jesus Christ, will then be caught up to meet Him in the air. Paul explains it this way.

After that, we who are still alive and are left will be caught up together with them in the clouds to meet the Lord in the air. And so we will be with the Lord forever (1 Thessalonians 4:17).

According to this promise there will be a generation of Christians who will never die. While the general rule is that each human being does eventually die such will not be the case here. Millions of believers in Jesus Christ will never see physical death.

10. THE LIVING BELIEVERS WILL RECEIVE NEW BODIES AT THAT TIME

Not only will these living believers be caught up to meet the Lord in the air, they too, like the resurrected saints, shall receive new bodies. Paul wrote.

> It will happen in a moment, in the blink of an eye, when the last trumpet is blown. For when the trumpet sounds, those who have died will be raised to live forever. And we who are living will also be transformed. For our dying bodies must be transformed into bodies that will never die; our mortal bodies must be transformed into immortal bodies. Then, when our dying bodies have been transformed into bodies that will never die, this Scripture will be fulfilled (1 Corinthians 15:52-54).

Like the believing dead, the living believers will receive a new body at this time. This new body will be immortal and incorruptible. It is important to understand that this new body will have some sort of continuity with the present body. In other words, this present body will be changed into a perfect body that will last for all eternity.

11. THIS WILL ALL HAPPEN IN A BLINK OF AN EYE

The translation of the church will occur instantaneously; in the twinkling of an eye. One moment the Christians are here while the next moment they are gone. Disappeared! Paul wrote about this to the Corinthians. He stated it as follows.

> In a flash, in the twinkling of an eye, at the last trumpet. For the trumpet will sound, the dead will be raised imperishable, and we will be changed (1 Corinthians 15:52).

This transformation will happen instantly. Every living believer in Jesus Christ will suddenly be gone. Those who have not believed will be left behind.

12. ALL OF THE BELIEVERS IN CHRIST, LIVING AND DEAD, WILL BE GATHERED TOGETHER

This event will bring all believers "in Christ" together. Loved ones will reunite. Death will no longer be a barrier because Jesus, as He promised, has come for those who have believed in Him. The church, which is called the bride and body of Christ, is now complete.

THESE BELIEVERS WILL FOREVER BE WITH THE LORD

The result of the rapture of living believers, and the resurrection of those who have died in Christ, is that all of us will forever be with the Lord. Paul wrote.

> After that, we who are still alive and are left will be caught up together with them in the clouds to meet the Lord in the air. And so we will be with the Lord forever (1 Thessalonians 4:17).

Believers will spend eternity with the Lord. This is the great truth of the rapture. Wherever He is, we will be!

THESE TRUTHS SHOULD BE A COMFORT FOR BELIEVERS

We learn that these truths should be comforting for all believers. Jesus told His disciples not to be troubled, or afraid, that He was going away.

> Do not let your hearts be troubled. Trust in God; trust also in me (John 14:1).

In fact, Paul said that we should "comfort" or "encourage" each other with these words. He wrote.

Therefore encourage one another with these words (1 Thessalonians 4:18).

The fact of Jesus coming back for His own is indeed a comfort for Christians. We have genuine hope for the future!

THESE TRUTHS ARE FOUNDATIONAL

These truths about the rapture of the church are our starting point in the examination of this doctrine. Now that we know what the Scripture has to say about this coming event, it is important that we begin to investigate other issues regarding the rapture; specifically, its timing. When will it occur with respect to the Second Coming of Christ to the earth? That is the question which needs to be answered.

SUMMARY TO QUESTION 3
WHAT SPECIFIC TRUTHS DO WE LEARN ABOUT THE RAPTURE FROM SCRIPTURE?

When we examine the three main passages that speak of the rapture of the church, John 14:1-3, First Thessalonians 4:13-18 and First Corinthians 15:50-58, we can make the following observations.

First, this doctrine about the rapture of the church is important for us to know. Paul wrote that he did not want the Thessalonians to be ignorant of this truth. Neither should we be ignorant. We need to know what the Bible has to say about this subject. We also find that while the Thessalonians could be sorrowful over those which had died, their sorrow was not to be like the unbelievers who have no hope. Christians have hope. Paul would go on to explain why the dead "in Christ" are not at a disadvantage to those who are alive.

Next we note that Paul emphasized that the truth of the rapture was specifically given by the Word of the Lord. Some believe that this refers to Jesus words recorded in the gospels; specifically in Matthew 24 and 25 when Jesus was speaking of His coming again to the earth.

However, there is nothing in the Olivet Discourse that clearly explains the rapture of the church. It is possible Paul could have been writing about certain oral teachings of Jesus which were not recorded in the gospels. More likely, Paul is talking about direct revelation given to him by the Lord.

In the gospel of John we find that Jesus said that He had to leave His disciples. Though He was going away He promised that someday He would return for His own. This speaks of the rapture of the church. Jesus said He is presently preparing a place for those who have believed in Him. Though Jesus spoke of coming back for His own, He did not elaborate on the details. This privilege was given to the Apostle Paul. The doctrine of the rapture was a mystery, or sacred secret, that Paul explained to the believers.

As far as the event itself, the rapture of the church begins with the Lord Jesus descending from heaven. He leaves the glory of heaven to bring believers to Himself. When He leaves heaven Jesus will give a loud shout or command. This will set the stage for the resurrection of believers. Interestingly, the gospels contain two illustrations of shouts, or loud cries, from Jesus which resulted in certain dead people coming back to life. One was at the tomb of Lazarus and the other was when He died on the cross. Each time when Jesus shouted out people came back to life. We are also told that the voice of Jesus is like that of an archangel. In other words, it is a powerful sound which He makes.

Trumpets are used in Scripture to signify important events. Paul said that the trumpet of God shall sound when Jesus descends from heaven. This is a further illustration of the magnitude of the occasion. After the Lord descends from heaven, those who have died "in Christ" will be raised with new bodies. Their mortal bodies will become immortal; the corruptible bodies will become incorruptible.

The living believers will then be caught up to meet the Lord in the air, or raptured. They will disappear from the sight of those left behind.

Consequently these believers will be exceptions to the rule that everyone must die once; these Christians will never experience physical death. Like the dead which have just been raised with new bodies, the living believers will be given their new bodies at that time. These bodies will be immortal and imperishable. Thus, there will be a gathering together of all the believers "in Christ;" those who have died and those who are alive. It will be a great time of reunion.

All of this will happen in a twinkling of an eye. As fast as an eye can blink, this event will take place. In other words, it is instantaneous. One moment the believers are here, the next moment they are all gone. From this time forward, these believers "in Christ" will forever be with the Lord. This fulfills Jesus' promise to His disciples. Before Jesus left this world He said He would come for His own people. This will be fulfilled at the rapture of the church.

These truths should be used by believers to comfort one another. Indeed, knowing these things should provide a legitimate hope for those who have trusted Christ. In sum these are the simple truths which the Bible states about the rapture, or translation, of the church. From them, we can further build the New Testament doctrine of the rapture.

QUESTION 4

What Are Some "Do's and Don'ts" That We Should Keep In Mind When Studying The Subject Of The Rapture?

The "rapture" refers to the doctrine that the church, the true believers in Jesus Christ, will be "caught up" from the earth to meet the Lord in the air. Again we emphasize that this refers to the genuine believers in Jesus; not merely people who attend church or have some family background in Christianity.

At that time their physical bodies will be transformed from natural, corruptible and mortal bodies to spiritual, incorruptible, and immortal bodies. These raptured believers will forever be in the presence of the Lord.

While the Bible teaches that such an event will take place there is disagreement among Bible believers as to its *timing*. Therefore, it is important that we have an understanding of the various ways in which Christians view this issue.

However, before we look into the question of the timing of the rapture of the church there are a number of preliminary matters which need to be addressed. Indeed, there are a number of "do's and don'ts" which need to be stressed when examining this question. They are as follows.

1. WE NEED TO CORRECTLY FRAME THE ISSUE

Any question regarding the rapture of the church must be properly stated or "framed." It is important that we understand the precise issues as well as why people hold to the various positions which they embrace.

Therefore, whether we agree with them or not, we should take the time to know why each position believes what they believe. Consequently, we must examine the *best* arguments which are put forward for each side.

This being the case it will not do to find the weakest arguments for one particular point of view and then attempt to refute them. On the contrary we should attempt to find the most persuasive arguments which each side offers and then interact with them. The fact that some people have offered poor or simplistic arguments in the past should not be an issue. We don't want to seek out the worst arguments each side proposes. Instead we want to find the best. Only then can we come to a proper conclusion on the matter.

Therefore, we should not cite only selective verses or passages which promote *our* particular position while deliberately ignoring other passages which may contradict what we believe. Full disclosure is absolutely essential.

2. WE SHOULD NOT PREDETERMINE THE OUTCOME OF OUR STUDY

In looking at this question, as to what the Bible teaches about the rapture of the church, our goal should be to discover the *truth* of the matter. Thus, the outcome should not be pre-determined before we examine all of the evidence. If the evidence leads us to a different position than what we have previously held, then we must change our position; we should not try to change the evidence! While this may not be easy to do it is something that must be done if we are going to be intellectually honest.

3. WE MUST PUT THIS QUESTION INTO PROPER PERSPECTIVE

Once we understand this issue we must then put it into proper perspective. There are two extremes in which we must avoid. The first sees this matter of the rapture of the church as of little or no importance. Basically, people who hold this view look at the question of the rapture and its timing as irrelevant to everyday life. There are more important matters which deserve our attention. Thus, this biblical doctrine receives little or no consideration.

The other extreme sees this doctrine as primary; it is one of the central beliefs of the faith. The timing of the rapture is placed alongside the Person and work of Jesus Christ, the nature of the Bible and the doctrine of salvation as an essential point of Christian teaching.

Neither of these extreme approaches is correct. The answer lies somewhere in the middle.

As we noted in an earlier question, we will find that this issue is certainly not irrelevant. If the believers are taken out of the world before the time when God's wrath is poured out on humanity, then we should be looking to the coming of Christ to deliver us from this period.

On the other hand, if Christians are going to experience this horrific time, and suffer to some degree with the unbelievers, then we must prepare for such a period. Consequently, believers in Christ will conduct themselves differently depending upon their view of the timing of the rapture of the church. This issue is not unimportant.

Having said this we do not want to go to the other extreme. As we examine the New Testament we do not find the timing of the rapture as being the prime focus of the preaching and teaching of Christ and His apostles. Indeed, apart from a few specific references, we do not find the issue of the rapture of the church mentioned at all. Therefore, the key is to try and find the right balance when studying and discussing this issue. This is not always easy to do.

4. WE MUST NOT MAKE THIS ISSUE A TEST OF FELLOWSHIP

This cannot be stressed too strongly. After our study of this subject, or perhaps even before we have made a serious study of the topic, we may have a view which we sincerely and deeply hold. There is nothing wrong with this.

However, what is wrong is to make our particular view the basis on which we associate with other Christians. While it is probably important that we go to a particular church that holds the same view as we do on this subject, it is certainly not essential. This is an important matter but there are a number of other issues which are of greater importance. The timing of the rapture is not the gospel! This should never be forgotten.

5. WE MUST REALIZE THAT THERE ARE NO QUICK, EASY ANSWERS TO THIS ISSUE

No particular view of end-time events is without problems. Thus, as far as coming to conclusions about the timing of the rapture is concerned, we must understand that there is no simple answer to this question, neither is there any quick solution. If there were then all Christians would be in agreement on this topic. The fact that godly men and women disagree on this matter should make this clear.

Almost everyone agrees that there is no single verse or passage that gives an undeniable or irrefutable answer to this question of the timing of the rapture. Any answer must be derived from studying the totality of Scripture. We cannot pick one verse here and another verse there in an attempt to construct this doctrine. It is an issue that demands our serious study.

Furthermore, any conclusion that is arrived at must be able to account for *all* of the objections brought against it. The theory must be able to give reasonable answers to specific questions.

As we have already indicated, we are convinced that the Pre-Tribulation theory is the view that best fits with all of the facts. While we believe that the Pre-Tribulation rapture view is the correct position we are well aware that godly people can and do disagree with our conclusion. Indeed, some individuals may use the same facts to come to an entirely different conclusion. Again we want to emphasize that we have no problem with this.

6. WE MUST NOT THINK WE HAVE ALL THE ANSWERS TO THIS QUESTION

While this point can be applied to any biblical subject under discussion it seems especially appropriate here. Too many people claim to have all the answers with respect to the question of the timing of the rapture. This includes people on every side of this issue!

Obviously everyone cannot be correct as to the timing of this coming event. Somebody has to be wrong. Human nature is such that *we* think *we* have the correct answer while the other person has the wrong answer. While that may indeed be the case, it is also possible that the other person has the correct answer and we are the ones which are wrong! We always have to allow for this possibility.

Even if we believe we have the correct answer on this question it is still our Christian duty to graciously and lovingly treat others who disagree with our conclusions. We should not assume that we are more intelligent or more spiritual than those who hold differing perspectives.

Unfortunately, there is way too much name-calling going on from people on all sides of this issue. This should not be our approach in tackling this question. We need to discuss the issues surrounding this event with a large dose of Christian charity. This is what pleases the Lord.

7. SCRIPTURE ALONE MUST BE OUR GUIDE

This last point is crucial. What solves this question is not what certain people may have taught in the history of the church or what we think current events may be telling us. While we may look at what others in the past have said about this issue, as well as what is presently going on in the world, the ultimate authority is the Scripture and the Scripture alone.

Every conclusion concerning the doctrine of the rapture of the church must come from the Bible and only from the Bible. The teaching of God's Word on this subject is the only thing which really matters.

These "do's and don'ts" should be kept in mind as we go about examining this particular issue, the rapture of the church.

SUMMARY TO QUESTION 4
WHAT ARE SOME "DO'S AND DON'TS" THAT WE SHOULD KEEP IN MIND WHEN STUDYING THE SUBJECT OF THE RAPTURE?

The rapture or translation of the church speaks of a time when the Lord snatches up the true believers in Jesus Christ who are on the earth and immediately brings them into His presence. In a moment, in a blink of an eye, they are changed from mortal, sinful beings to immortal beings with a perfect glorified body. These raptured believers will forever be with the Lord.

While this doctrine is taught in Scripture, there are many issues regarding the rapture of the church in which Bible-believers are divided. Indeed, there is no consensus of opinion about this event. This being the case there are a number of important things we should take notice of as we approach our study of this issue.

First, we should attempt to understand or frame this issue the best way in which we can. In other words, we should do our best to correctly understand why people have differing points of view. Thus, we must look at the most convincing arguments each position offers and make our decision as to what we believe based upon the best evidence available.

In doing so, we should be intellectually honest and not pre-determine our conclusion before we examine all the facts. If we discover the facts contradict a position we have previously held, then we need to go with the facts.

Next, we should have this issue in proper perspective. It is important as to what we will conclude about the timing of the rapture because, among other things, it will affect the way in which we conduct our Christian life as well as prepare for the future. The timing of the rapture is not an irrelevant issue.

On the other hand, it is *not* the gospel. The Great Commission from Jesus Christ is that we preach the good news about Him and teach His truth to all nations. This message is that He had died for the sins of the world, was buried, and that He rose from the dead three days later. Forgiveness of sin only comes from Him. This is the message Jesus commanded us to proclaim. Thus, we must put this matter of the rapture of the church into proper perspective giving it the right amount of attention it deserves.

While we may have a particular conviction as to which view of the timing of the rapture is correct, we should not make our position as a determining factor as to which Christians we will, or will not, associate with. All true Christians are our brothers and our sisters and should be treated as such. We should not have an "us versus them" mentality when it comes to this topic.

We should also realize that there are no easy answers to this question. Indeed, if there were a simple answer then all Christians would be in agreement. The fact that they are not unified in this matter should keep us humble when we discuss the issue with others.

No matter how much we understand about this topic there are always new things we can learn. The issues are complex. Consequently we should not think that we have all the answers. We never will. That is why we must keep on studying God's Word!

Whatever position we ultimately decide to take on this subject, it is important that we should treat others who see things differently graciously and with Christian love. There is no place for name-calling when discussing this topic. None whatsoever! The Lord is pleased only when issues such as these are discussed in a Christlike manner. This should be our goal.

Finally, this issue can only be decided from the teachings of the Bible. No outside source should be given equal authority. Thus, while it is proper to discover what those in the history of the church may have said about this topic, or what current events may be telling us, the only thing which really matters is what God's Word says. On this basis alone, this question must be decided.

What Is The Relationship Of The Rapture To The 70th Week Of Daniel?

One of the key questions with respect to the timing of the rapture of the church is how it fits in with the prophecy of the "seventy weeks of Daniel;" particularly with the last or "seventieth week."

In fact, how one interprets the prophecy of Daniel's seventy weeks will usually determine how one views the timing of the rapture of the church. This makes correctly interpreting Daniel's prophecy of the utmost importance. We can illustrate this as follows.

THE GREAT PROPHECY OF THE SEVENTY WEEKS OF DANIEL

Daniel the prophet had been praying about the future of the nation Israel. The Bible says that he was visited by the angel Gabriel who gave him this prophecy of the "seventy sevens" or "seventy weeks." It reads as follows.

> Seventy 'sevens' are decreed for your people and your holy city to finish transgression, to put an end to sin, to atone for wickedness, to bring in everlasting righteousness, to seal up vision and prophecy and to anoint the Most Holy Place. Know and understand this: From the time the word goes out to restore and rebuild Jerusalem until the Anointed One, the ruler, comes, there will be seven "sevens," and sixty-two "sevens." It will be rebuilt with streets and a trench, but in

times of trouble. After the sixty-two "sevens," the Anointed One will be put to death and will have nothing. The people of the ruler who will come will destroy the city and the sanctuary. The end will come like a flood: War will continue until the end, and desolations have been decreed. He will confirm a covenant with many for one 'seven.' In the middle of the 'seven' he will put an end to sacrifice and offering. And at the temple he will set up an abomination that causes desolation, until the end that is decreed is poured out on him (Daniel 9:24-27).

From this prediction recorded in the Book of Daniel, we can make a number of observations. They are as follows.

1. THE PREDICTIONS CONCERNING ISRAEL'S FUTURE ARE DIVIDED INTO THREE PERIODS

Here we find that the future of the nation of Israel is laid out for us. Daniel is told it will be divided into three periods of "weeks," or "sevens." The first is seven weeks, or seven sevens, then sixty-two weeks, or sixty-two sevens, then one final week, or one seven. The sevens can be days, weeks, or years depending upon the context. Almost all commentators agree that the weeks, or sevens, are *years*.

Therefore, we are dealing with three periods of time. The first period is forty-nine years, the second period is four hundred and thirty-four years, and the final period is seven years. The total number of years is four hundred and ninety. At the end of this four hundred and ninety year period everlasting righteousness will prevail!

2. THE STARTING DATE IS GIVEN TO US

The time to begin to count the seventy sevens, or four hundred and ninety years, would be at a specific occurrence. We are told there would be a command given to restore and rebuild the city of Jerusalem. The fulfillment of this commandment is recorded in Nehemiah 2:1. When

Jerusalem was restored and rebuilt the first period of sevens, or forty-nine years, ended.

The next period of sevens, or four hundred and thirty-four years, brings us to the first century A.D. and to the life of Jesus Christ. There is discussion among biblical scholars as to exactly *when* this ended. Some argue it was at Jesus' baptism while others contend it was fulfilled at His triumphal entry into Jerusalem.

Whatever the case may be, the second group of "sevens," or four hundred and thirty-four years, were fulfilled *during* the life and ministry of Jesus Christ.

3. THERE IS AN INTERVAL BETWEEN THE SIXTY-NINTH AND SEVENTIETH WEEK

It is important to understand that the prophetic clock stopped during the life and ministry of Jesus Christ. Whether at His baptism or His triumphal entry the clock has now stopped. The four hundred and eighty-three years have ended. Daniel then wrote of certain events that would take place during an *interval period between* the sixty-ninth and seventieth week. We read the following.

> After the sixty-two 'sevens,' the Anointed One will be put to death and will have nothing. The people of the ruler who will come will destroy the city and the sanctuary. The end will come like a flood: War will continue until the end, and desolations have been decreed (Daniel 9:26)

Notice he speaks of particular events which will take place *after* the sixty-two sevens. This means there is an interval between the sixty-nine weeks (already fulfilled) and the future seventieth week. We are presently in that interval.

Daniel was told that during this interval two tragic events would take place. They are as follows.

4. THE MESSIAH WAS TO DIE DURING THE INTERVAL

The first event was that the promised Messiah would be killed after He arrived on the scene. Instead of establishing His kingdom at that time, He would die.

A. ISAIAH WROTE OF HIS DEATH

This prediction in Daniel, of the death of the Christ, fits well with the prophecies given to other prophets of God. The prophet Isaiah wrote that the Messiah would suffer.

We read the following prophetic words.

> Who has believed our message and to whom has the arm of the LORD been revealed? He grew up before him like a tender shoot, and like a root out of dry ground. He had no beauty or majesty to attract us to him, nothing in his appearance that we should desire him. He was despised and rejected by mankind, a man of suffering, and familiar with pain. Like one from whom people hide their faces he was despised, and we held him in low esteem. Surely he took up our pain and bore our suffering, yet we considered him punished by God, stricken by him, and afflicted. But he was pierced for our transgressions, he was crushed for our iniquities; the punishment that brought us peace was on him, and by his wounds we are healed. We all, like sheep, have gone astray, each of us has turned to our own way; and the LORD has laid on him the iniquity of us all. He was oppressed and afflicted, yet he did not open his mouth; he was led like a lamb to the slaughter, and as a sheep before its shearers is silent, so he did not open his mouth. By oppression and judgment he was taken away. Yet who of his generation protested? For he was cut off from the land of the living; for the transgression of my people he was punished. He was assigned a grave with the wicked, and with the rich in his death, though he had done no violence, nor was any deceit in his mouth (Isaiah 53:1-9).

Here are clear predictions of the suffering of the "Servant of the Lord;" the Christ or the Messiah. He will "take our pain," "bare our suffering," be "pierced for our transgressions," and "crushed for our iniquities," and by "his wounds we will be healed."

B. THE MESSIAH WILL BE PIERCED

Zechariah the prophet said that the Messiah would be "pierced." He made the following predictions.

> And I will pour out on the house of David and the inhabitants of Jerusalem a spirit of grace and supplication. They will look on me, the one they have pierced, and they will mourn for him as one mourns for an only child, and grieve bitterly for him as one grieves for a firstborn son (Zechariah 12:10).

Therefore, Daniel's prophecy, coupled with that of Isaiah and Zechariah, predicted the suffering and death of the Promised Messiah. The New Testament records the fulfillment of these predictions in the death of Jesus Christ.

5. THE CITY AND TEMPLE WERE TO BE DESTROYED DURING THE INTERVAL

The second tragedy involved the city of Jerusalem and the Holy Temple. Not only would the Messiah die, the city and the Temple would again be destroyed. The irony is that this prediction, recorded in the Book of Daniel, came soon after the destruction of the city and the *First* Temple.

As always, God is true to His Word. The Messiah, Jesus of Nazareth, was killed and shortly thereafter the city of Jerusalem and the Temple were destroyed again. The predictions have been fulfilled.

6. THE FUTURE SEVEN YEAR PERIOD

Today we are still in this interval period between the sixty-ninth and seventieth week of Daniel. As we have noted, there is one final week, or seven year period, which remains to be fulfilled. The prophecy is stated as follows.

> He will confirm a covenant with many for one 'seven.' In the middle of the 'seven' he will put an end to sacrifice and offering. And at the temple he will set up an abomination that causes desolation, until the end that is decreed is poured out on him (Daniel 9:27)

Thus, certain predicted events are going to be fulfilled in the future.

THE SEVENTIETH WEEK OF DANIEL AND THE GREAT TRIBULATION

The seventieth week of Daniel is also termed "the great tribulation." There are those who object uniting these two terms because they insist that the great tribulation does not encompass this entire seven year period. However, the term "great tribulation" has become a convenient term to describe this last seven year period rather than using the more cumbersome term "the seventieth week of Daniel." So we will use the terms interchangeably while recognizing that some do not equate the two.

THE CONFIRMATION BY JESUS OF THIS FUTURE PERIOD

As we have noted, it is necessary to have some type of gap between the end of the sixty-ninth week of Daniel and the start of the seventieth week. Indeed, the fact that the Messiah was to die and that the city and Temple were to be destroyed indicates that the seventieth week does not begin immediately after the sixty-ninth week.

We find this confirmed by the words of the Lord Jesus. When asked about "the sign" of His coming He said the following.

> So when you see standing in the holy place 'the abomination that causes desolation,' spoken of through the prophet Daniel--let the reader understand (Matthew 24:15).

According to Jesus, the abomination of desolation, which Daniel wrote about, was yet to be fulfilled. This speaks of a defiling of the Holy of Holies in the Temple. This is still future. In fact, it would be "the" sign that His return to the earth was near. This indicates there is still a seven-year period to be fulfilled with respect to the nation Israel.

THE BEGINNING OF THE LAST SEVEN YEARS: THE SEVENTIETH WEEK OF DANIEL

According to this prediction, the seventieth week of Daniel will begin with the signing of a peace treaty between the nation of Israel and a coming world ruler, the final Antichrist. Once this treaty has been signed, the prophetic clock begins to start. It is in this last seven-year period, the great tribulation, where many of the events recorded in the Book of Revelation take place.

THE SEVENTIETH WEEK OF DANIEL AND THE RAPTURE OF THE CHURCH

What does this have to do with the subject of the rapture of the church? If there is one last seven-year period of great distress or great tribulation that the earth will experience before the Second Coming of Jesus Christ then the question is, "Where does the rapture of the church fit within this time period?" Does it occur before this last seven-year period? Does it take place in the midst of the seven-year period, near the end of this period or at the very end of this final seven years? These are the questions that need to be answered.

Therefore, to be aware of issues surrounding the timing of the rapture we must understand Daniel's prophecy about one seven-year period which remains to be fulfilled before the Lord Jesus returns.

SUMMARY TO QUESTION 5
WHAT IS THE RELATIONSHIP OF THE RAPTURE TO THE 70TH WEEK OF DANIEL?

The prophecy of the "seventy weeks," or "seventy sevens" of Daniel is one of the most important in all of Scripture. Indeed, it details the history of the nation Israel from the time of the command to build the Second Temple, about 445 B.C., until the Second Coming of Jesus Christ. In addition, it may have specific things to teach us about the timing of the rapture of the church. Consequently, it is crucial that we have a proper understanding of what is predicted in this passage.

From a study of this prophecy we find that seventy sevens or seventy weeks are determined upon the people of Israel. At the end of these seventy weeks, the Lord will bring in everlasting righteousness. The weeks are periods of seven. They could be days, weeks or years. Almost all commentators understand them to be years.

Therefore, the prophecy of Daniel concerns four hundred and ninety years in which God deals with the nation Israel. These years are divided into three periods: seven weeks or forty-nine years, sixty-two weeks, or four hundred and thirty-four years, and one week, or seven years.

It is important to understand that these years are not consecutive. After the first two periods, or four hundred and eighty-three years in total, which are consecutive, the prophetic clock stopped. This occurred at some time during the life and ministry of Jesus Christ. The prophecy said that *after* the four hundred and eighty-three years, or sixty-nine weeks were finished, the Messiah would be killed, and the city of Jerusalem and the temple destroyed. This occurred exactly as predicted.

Therefore, one more week, or seven years, still remains where God deals with the nation of Israel before the return of Christ. This period is known as the seventieth week of Daniel or the Great Tribulation. It will be a time of unparalleled trouble.

This seventieth week will begin when a peace treaty is signed or confirmed between the nation of Israel and a coming world ruler. This signing of the treaty will start the countdown of the last seven years before the return of the Lord.

It is argued that since the last seven-year period deals specifically with the nation Israel, then the New Testament church does not have to be around at that time. God will be finished with the church, the true believers in Jesus Christ. Consequently, the Lord will then turn His attention again to His chosen people, Israel. This perspective understands a biblical distinction between the people of Israel and the New Testament church.

Hence the rapture of the church must occur before this last seven year period begins. Once the church has been removed, then the final week of Daniel's prophecy can commence. This is further evidence that the rapture of the church must occur before the last seven year period leading up to the Second Coming of Christ.

What Are The Various Views That Bible-Believers Hold Regarding The Timing Of The Rapture?

Bible-believers are not in agreement as to the timing of the rapture of the church. Indeed, there are five major views which are held by Christians as to when the rapture will take place. Furthermore, some believers do not think that such an event as a "rapture" will ever take place! Other Christians acknowledge the rapture will occur but they do not think there is sufficient information given to us in the Scripture about the timing of this event.

For now, we will briefly state these positions. In the next few questions we will look at each theory in-depth. Simply stated, they are as follows.

OPTION 1: THERE IS NO RAPTURE

There are some Christians who deny such an event as the rapture of the church will take place. They claim that there will be no future episode where the Lord gathers up the believers to meet Him in the air. Those who hold this perspective believe the passages referring to the rapture have been wrongly interpreted. They contend believers will remain *upon the earth* until Christ comes again. Consequently, Christians should not be looking for the Lord to snatch them away in the rapture.

OPTION 2: THE RAPTURE IS ONLY FOR SPIRITUAL CHRISTIANS

According to this theory the issue is not the timing of the event but the subjects of the event. It is called the "Partial Rapture" theory because it is thought that not all true Christians will be taken up to meet the Lord in the air. Only those who are prepared, or spiritually worthy, will be caught up to meet the Lord in the rapture of the church.

This view comes in more than one form. There are those who believe the partial rapture will take place at different times, and in different groups, before Jesus Christ comes back to the earth. The first rapture will occur before the great tribulation then other believers in Christ will be raptured at various intervals during the tribulation based upon their spiritual worthiness.

Others who hold this position assume there will be only one rapture event. Those who miss the catching away of the church will have to endure the sufferings of the great tribulation.

Though this view comes in more than one form, all who hold this position agree that not every true Christian will be taken up to meet the Lord when the rapture occurs. In other words, there will be some Christians left behind.

OPTION 3: THE PRE-TRIBULATION RAPTURE THEORY

There are many who believe the rapture will take place before the beginning of the great tribulation; the final seven-year period before the coming of Christ. This theory is known as the "Pre-Tribulation" rapture view. According to this position, believers will escape the unprecedented time of God's wrath which will come upon the earth. These Christians will return with the Lord in triumph at the end of the seven-year period. As we have mentioned, this is the viewpoint which is adopted in this book.

OPTION 4: THE MID-TRIBULATION RAPTURE THEORY

There are those who believe the rapture will take place in the middle of the final seven-year period before Jesus Christ returns to the earth. Before the wrath of God is poured out upon the people living on the earth, the church will be taken away to meet the Lord in the rapture. This is known as the "Mid-Tribulation" view.

OPTION 5: THE PRE-WRATH RAPTURE VIEW

There is a recent view that believes the rapture will take place three-fourths of the way through the final seven-year period. However, it will occur before the wrath of God comes to the earth. This is known as the "Pre-Wrath" rapture view. It differs from the Mid-Tribulation rapture in that it occurs later in time. It also differs from the Post-Tribulation view in that the rapture does not occur at the very end of the seventieth week of Daniel. Thus, the Pre-Wrath rapture has the rapture occurring some five and one half years into the seven-year tribulation period.

OPTION 6: THE POST-TRIBULATION RAPTURE THEORY

There are Christians who believe the rapture will take place at the very end of the seven-year great tribulation. Immediately before the Lord returns to set up His kingdom upon the earth, the church will be caught up to meet Him. They will join Christ as He returns to judge the wicked. This is known as the "Post-Tribulation" rapture view. This is the only theory which does not see a long interval between the rapture of the church and the Second Coming of Christ.

OPTION 7: THE BIBLE TEACHES THE RAPTURE BUT NOBODY CAN BE CERTAIN ABOUT THE TIMING

This last position says that while the rapture of the church is a biblical doctrine, the living believers will indeed be caught up at some time to meet the Lord in the air, there is not enough information given in Scripture so as to determine when this event will occur. The Bible tells us that the coming of the Lord is our hope, and this coming for the Christians is real. However, Scripture hasn't given us enough specifics to know exactly when this will happen.

According to this position, while we should teach the fact of the rapture of the church, we should not attempt to discover the timing of this event with respect to the Second Coming of Christ.

For His own reasons, God has not provided that information to us. Consequently, it is fruitless to argue about the timing of the rapture because it is not possible for us to know when it will occur with respect to the final seven-year period before the Lord returns; the seventieth week of Daniel.

RESPONSE: GOD DOES WANT US TO KNOW!

We will not evaluate this last position in a separate question. Instead, we will merely make a few brief points.

THERE IS SUFFICIENT INFORMATION IN SCRIPTURE

First, we believe that the Lord has given us sufficient information to understand *when* the rapture of the church will take place. Indeed, as we examine the totality of Scripture we will find this to be the case.

WHY WOULD THE LORD NOT WANT US TO KNOW?

In addition, we do not think the Lord would highlight such an important doctrine as the rapture and then not answer the question as to its timing. Why even mention it to the believers at all if we are not able to understand when it will occur according to His prophetic timetable?

THE TESTIMONY OF THE BOOK OF DANIEL

Finally, the Bible says that the understanding of prophetic matters will be clearer as we get near the end. We read in Daniel.

> But you, Daniel, roll up and seal the words of the scroll until the time of the end. Many will go here and there to increase knowledge (Daniel 12:4).

Daniel is told that these matters will be understood at the "time of the end." The knowledge that will increase is knowledge about prophecies concerning the "last days."

Then, after hearing angelic figures discussing matters concerning the time of the end, Daniel said the following.

> I heard, but I did not understand. So I asked, "My lord, what will the outcome of all this be?" He replied, "Go your way, Daniel, because the words are rolled up and sealed until the time of the end" (Daniel 12:8-9)

Notice that Daniel is again told that some matters will only make sense "at the time of the end." That is why he could not understand the meaning of what they were saying. We then read this statement.

> Many will be purified, made spotless and refined, but the wicked will continue to be wicked. None of the wicked will understand, but those who are wise will understand (Daniel 12:10).

We find that there will be people who understand what is taking place at the time of the end. While these verses refer specifically to the nation of Israel and its future, the principle is clear; as we get closer to end of the age more and more things written in Scripture will become clearer. We believe this includes the doctrine of the rapture as well as its timing.

Thus, we reject the idea that we cannot know when the rapture will take place in the prophetic timetable of the last days.

EACH VIEW IS HELD BY BIBLE-BELIEVERS

To sum up, each of these views is held by people who are Bible-believing Christians. Furthermore the advocates of these theories use Scripture to support their conclusions. This being the case we need to take a look at each theory and see which one best fits the facts.

In doing so, we will attempt to state the very best case we can put together for each particular view. We will then raise the popular objections to the theory. This way we can present, in a fair way, what each position claims as well as the biblical objections which have been brought up against each particular theory. Therefore, everyone will have an understanding of the strengths and weaknesses of each view.

Again, as we have noted, we will conclude that the Pre-Tribulation rapture position is the one we believe best fits with the totality of Scripture. However, even though we hold this view, we will do our very best to present the strongest arguments we can find for the other views.

SUMMARY TO QUESTION 6
WHAT ARE THE VARIOUS VIEWS THAT BIBLE-BELIEVERS HOLD REGARDING THE TIMING OF THE RAPTURE?

The doctrine of the rapture or the translation of the church is taught in Scripture. The Bible says there will be a time when living believers will be caught up to meet the Lord in the air. Immediately before this occurs, the believing dead will be raised.

When this glorious event comes to pass then all believers, living and dead will be given an immortal incorruptible body. Thus, at some future time, believers, living and dead will be united with Jesus Christ in new bodies. While Bible-believers, with few exceptions, agree that such an event will take place, the time of the occurrence of the rapture is one of disagreement between Christians. We can sum up the various views as follows. Some Christians actually deny that such an event as the rapture will happen. These people basically have to spiritualize the teaching of Scripture on this subject. They reject any literal interpretation of the passages which are used to support this idea.

Those who accept the biblical teaching of the rapture can be placed into one of five categories with respect to the timing of the event as well as who is to be taken in the rapture.

The partial rapture theory is more about who is to be taken rather than the timing. Indeed, it believes that not all Christians will meet the Lord in the air at the same time. Only when a believer is worthy will he or she be taken to meet the Lord. Not everyone who has trusted Christ is guaranteed to be taken up to meet the Lord. The Christian must be living in a manner which is worthy of the Lord to participate in the rapture.

Most Christians hold the view that when the rapture occurs everyone who has believed in Christ will be taken up to meet Him. Those who believe that all genuine Christians will be raptured do not all agree as to the timing of the event. There are four popular theories as to the timing.

Many Christians hold to the idea that the rapture will occur before the Great Tribulation period; the final seven years before Christ returns. The final seven-year period is also known as the "seventieth week of Daniel." The view, known as the pretribulation rapture, believes the church will be taken out of the world before any of the events of this period occur. Thus, according to this position, seven years before Christ returns to the earth, the church, the true believers in Jesus Christ, will be raptured or caught up to meet the Lord in the air.

Others see the rapture occurring during the midpoint of the seventieth week of Daniel, or the Great Tribulation period. This is known as the mid-tribulation rapture view. Thus, the position says that the rapture will occur three and a half years before the Second Coming of Christ.

A relatively new theory, the pre-wrath rapture, holds that sometime during the seventieth week of Daniel but before the wrath of God comes upon the people of the earth, the rapture will occur. This view holds that the rapture will take place about five and one half years into the seven year period of tribulation.

There is also the view that the church will experience the entire period of the Great Tribulation. The rapture will occur at the very end of the seventieth week of Daniel. This is known as the posttribulation rapture view. According to this perspective believers will be caught up to meet the Lord in the air as He returns to judge His enemies and set up His kingdom.

Also, there are some who believe the rapture of the church is taught in Scripture but the exact timing is not made clear to us. While at some future time the living believers will meet the Lord in the air and will be with Him forever, we cannot know for certain when this will happen because the Lord has not made this matter clear. Therefore, we should not spend time arguing about the timing of this event because God has decided not to reveal it to us. We reject this view for a few basic reasons. First, God has revealed the doctrine of the rapture in Scripture and has given us sufficient information with respect to its timing.

Second, it would be odd that after revealing this momentous event that is to come the Lord would not give us any indication as to how it fits in with the "last days" scenario. We would expect Him to do this and we believe that He has. Finally, in the last chapter of the Book of Daniel the prophet is specifically told that knowledge about prophetic matters will increase at the time of the end. We believe this includes an understanding of the timing of the rapture. In sum, there are good Christians who hold each of these views. The important thing is to determine exactly what the Bible says on this matter. This can only be done by giving a fair hearing to each viewpoint and looking at its strengths and weaknesses.

QUESTION 7

Should We Attempt To Attribute Motives As To Why Certain Positions On The Rapture Are Held?

Before we examine the various positions which are held with respect to the rapture of the church there is another introductory matter which should be discussed. We often find people attributing motives to those who hold differing views with respect to the timing of the rapture. Should this be done? Should anyone attempt to discover *why* people hold to a particular position? Does their motivation really matter?

Too often we find those holding the various views of the rapture being characterized as having some improper motivation. While motivations are often attributed to those holding opposing views, this is one thing we should not ever do! Thus, we need to make the following observations.

1. THE NO RAPTURE VIEW IS NOT HELD BY PEOPLE WHO DOUBT THE BIBLE

There are godly Bible-believing people who hold the "no-rapture" view. Nobody should question their integrity. They have convictions that this is what the Scripture teaches on the subject.

Some hold this view because they believe prophetic passages should be spiritualized rather than being taken literally. This may be a valid point of disagreement among Bible-believers.

Yet too often those holding this view are accused of either denying God's Word, of minimizing Scripture, or of being closet unbelievers. This is unfair.

THE PARTIAL RAPTURE IS NOT HELD BECAUSE PEOPLE THINK THEY ARE MORE SPIRITUAL

In addition, there are many godly people, past and present, who have held the "partial rapture" position. They have come to this conclusion through their own understanding of Scripture. If we assume they are incorrect in their beliefs then we should not do so based upon any motives we think they may have. There should be no characterization of these Christians as considering themselves to be the "spiritually elite."

PRE-TRIBULATIONISM IS NOT HELD BECAUSE CHRISTIANS WISH TO ESCAPE COMING TROUBLES

One thing which should be clearly stated about the Pre-Tribulation view is that it is *not* held merely because believers want to escape trouble or have an easier life. Unfortunately, this accusation gets hurled too often at those who believe the Scripture teaches the Pre-Tribulation rapture. Such charges are unfair and untrue. The great majority of people who have looked at the issue of the timing of the rapture of the church, and have come to the conclusion that the church will escape the great tribulation, do so because of their conviction that the Scriptures teach this to be a fact.

Consequently it is wrong as well as uncharitable to attribute other motives to such people.

MID-TRIBULATIONISM IS NOT HELD BECAUSE PEOPLE WANT TO COMPROMISE

Mid-Tribulationism accepts some of the truths of Pre-Tribulationism and some of Post-Tribulationism. Likewise it rejects certain of the arguments each position puts forward. Consequently, some have accused those of holding Mid-Tribulationism as people who do not wish to take sides. Thus, they claim that the Mid-Trib supporters compromise their beliefs.

This is an unfair way to look at this view. Those who have embraced this position have done so because it is their understanding of what the Scripture says on the topic. While this position may be incorrect biblically, it should not be challenged based upon what somebody thinks motivates those who hold this view.

THE PRE-WRATH POSITION IS NOT HELD BECAUSE PEOPLE WANT TO BELIEVE SOMETHING NEW

The Pre-Wrath position is new. Because it is the latest view put forward as to the timing of the rapture it is rightly challenged. However, we should not challenge the motives of those which hold this view. In other words, we should not assume these people are trying to come up with some "new doctrine" or "new belief."

The view may be new but this does not necessarily mean that it is wrong. If it is wrong then the facts will make it clear. Thus, this option should not be rejected out of hand merely because of its newness. Indeed, it should only be rejected if it does not match up to Scripture.

6. POST-TRIBULATIONISM IS NOT HELD BECAUSE SOME PEOPLE WANT TO SUFFER

It is unfair to claim that those who believe the church will go through the tribulation, the Post-Tribulation position, have some sort of martyr complex. Those who embrace the Post-Tribulation view are certainly not looking forward to the terrible things which Scripture says will come upon those dwelling on the earth. They hold this position because they sincerely believe this is what the Bible teaches on the subject. Everyone should respect their belief.

SCRIPTURE MUST BE THE FINAL DETERMINER OF THE TRUTH

This is a sampling of some of the unfair criticisms which each of these rapture positions receive. Again we emphasize that the correct view of this issue must be decided from the teachings of Scripture alone. What may or may not motivate individuals to hold a particular view should not enter into the discussion.

With this in mind, let us now examine each of the major theories concerning the "rapture of the church."

SUMMARY TO QUESTION 7
SHOULD WE ATTEMPT TO ATTRIBUTE MOTIVES AS TO WHY CERTAIN POSITIONS ON THE RAPTURE ARE HELD?

There are some who wish to settle the question of the timing of the rapture of the church based upon what they think motivates those of other viewpoints. Instead of squarely facing the issues, the conclusions are founded upon what is seemingly wrong with the motivation of all others.

This happens much too often in this debate and it is clearly wrong. In doing our study of the rapture of the church, we should not attempt to attribute motives as to why people hold positions other than ours. This has been done too often and it should immediately stop. We should note the following about each of the rapture views.

The people who believe Scripture does not teach such an event as the rapture are often characterized as being those which deny God's truth, and such, must not be believers. However, many of those which hold this particular position have a view of prophecy that sees it as needing to be interpreted spiritually rather than literally. We can certainly disagree with their conclusions. Yet, in doing so, we should not assume that all of these people belittle the Word of God. That is an unfair characterization. Any opposition to this view must be based upon the correct understanding of what Scripture teaches on this subject; not on what we think may motivate the person holding the view.

Partial rapturism believes that not every believer has the promise of being caught up to meet the Lord when He comes for His church. Those who hold this view sincerely believe this is what Scripture teaches on the subject. They should not be unfairly characterized as those who think they are spiritually superior to others. Their case is made from the Bible and the truth of their assertions must be evaluated in light of Scripture.

Those who hold the pre-tribulation view are often characterized as people who want an easy life; those who do not want to suffer for the cause of Christ. Consequently, they embrace this view as a way of escaping the things predicted to come upon the earth. This is an unfair way of explaining why this view is held. The people who accept this view do so because they believe this is what the Scripture teaches on the subject.

The mid-tribulation view is sometimes characterized by a certain willingness to compromise rather than face the choices offered by the pre-tribulation and post-tribulation views. Again, this is the wrong way to look at their position. We should not assume these people want to avoid conflict and thus take a compromising position. This is an unfair way of assessing their claims.

The pre-wrath rapture is often looked down upon because it is the latest attempt to answer the question of the timing of the rapture. Those promoting the view are sometimes accused of presenting some "new truth" and, as such, should not be believed. Again, the accuracy of what they say should be decided on the merits of the argument and not upon what we think motivates people.

The people who hold the post-tribulation view are not people who have some sort of martyr complex or who enjoy suffering. They do not want to suffer or go through the suffering the world will receive in the future. Neither is their view mainly the result of tearing down other views. They sincerely believe this is what the Bible teaches on the subject.

These stereotypes about all the rapture positions should be once-and for-all done away with. Good Bible-believing people differ on this issue mainly because their study of the Scripture has led them to certain convictions.

In sum, we should never attribute to them ungodly motives as to why they reached their conclusions. Their conclusion may be wrong, but let us demonstrate where they are incorrect through the teachings of Scripture.

QUESTION 8

Why Do Some Bible-Believers Contend There Is No Such Thing As A Rapture? (The No Rapture Theory)

A great number of Bible-believers accept the doctrine of the rapture of the church; that the Lord will one day descend from heaven and "snatch away" all living believers in Jesus Christ to meet Him in the air. At that same time those believers which have died "in Christ" will be resurrected and will also meet the Lord with the living saints.

However, not everybody who is a Bible-believer holds to this idea. Indeed, there are those who do not believe that the rapture of the church will ever occur. The "no rapture" view says that the rapture of the church, as is commonly believed and taught, is a myth. They claim that there will be no such event.

Indeed, they do not think that the rapture of the church is a biblical doctrine when the Bible is rightly understood and interpreted. Those holding to this particular position declare that there is a scriptural basis for their belief. Therefore, they believe that they have the Bible on their side. They usually argue in the following way.

THE WORD RAPTURE IS NOT FOUND IN THE BIBLE

Often the first point raised in the "no rapture" theory is the claim that the word "rapture" is not found in the Bible. Since we do not find the word in the New Testament, it is claimed that the doctrine of the rapture of the church is not a biblical idea.

In addition, they also say that the passages which supposedly teach the rapture are misinterpreted. Once the Bible is properly understood it is contended that the idea of an event called the rapture will vanish.

Therefore, believers in Jesus Christ should not expect to someday be removed from this world by means of a supernatural "catching up" to meet the Lord.

THE LORD JESUS PRAYED TO KEEP BELIEVERS IN THE WORLD

Another reason the doctrine of the rapture of the church is denied is that it is against the specific prayer of the Lord Jesus in the Garden of Gethsemane. He prayed the following.

> My prayer is not that you take them out of the world but
> that you protect them from the evil one (John 17:15).

Jesus specifically asked God the Father that believers would *not* be taken out of the world but rather kept in it. Therefore, while the Lord Jesus is indeed coming again, He will *not* come back to take Christians away from the tribulation or suffering they have to experience.

Furthermore, this prayer was not merely for those disciples who were alive during His earthly ministry. In fact, we find that it was also for those who would come afterward. Jesus later prayed.

> My prayer is not for them alone. I pray also for those who
> will believe in me through their message (John 17:20).

Therefore, if Jesus, God the Son, asked God the Father to keep believers in this world and not to take them out, then the believers in Christ will not be taken out. It's that simple.

BELIEVERS DO NOT ESCAPE SUFFERING OR TRIBULATION

There is also the argument from the "suffering church." The rapture of the church removes believers from suffering and tribulation. This, it is argued, is not what the Bible says happens to those who trust Christ.

Indeed, from the beginning of the Scripture until the end, there are numerous passages which speak of true believers in the God of the Bible undergoing suffering.

For instance, righteous Job suffered the loss of all things. He was not removed from his state of suffering. To the contrary, he learned many lessons through his ordeal.

The patriarch Joseph was not immediately delivered from prison. In fact, he remained there for many years though he was innocent of any crime. This righteous man suffered.

BELIEVERS CAN BE PROTECTED DURING TIMES OF JUDGMENT

There is something else which should be considered. While there are examples of godly people suffering unjustly, there are also examples of the Lord Himself protecting His people in the midst of trouble. The Bible gives the following illustrations.

ISRAEL WAS PROTECTED FROM THE PLAGUES

The nation of Israel was not removed from the plagues in Egypt but rather they were protected through them. For example, we read about the plague that was put upon the livestock.

And the next day the LORD did it: All the livestock of the Egyptians died, but not one animal belonging to the Israelites died (Exodus 9:6).

In the same way, believers during the great tribulation can be protected from the wrath of God which is aimed at the unbelievers.

DANIEL'S FRIENDS WERE PROTECTED WITHIN THE FIERY FURNACE

Daniel's three friends were protected in the fiery furnace prepared by King Nebuchadnezzar. Indeed, they were *not* removed from it. We read about this in the Book of Daniel. The Bible says.

Nebuchadnezzar then approached the opening of the blazing furnace and shouted, "Shadrach, Meshach and Abednego, servants of the Most High God, come out! Come here!" So Shadrach, Meshach and Abednego came out of the fire, and the satraps, prefects, governors and royal advisers crowded around them. They saw that the fire had not harmed their bodies, nor was a hair of their heads singed; their robes were not scorched, and there was no smell of fire on them (Daniel 3:26-27).

Likewise, the believers in Jesus Christ can receive God's protection during the time of His wrath.

DANIEL WAS PROTECTED FROM HARM IN THE LION'S DEN

Daniel the prophet was *protected* in the lion's den when thrown in by King Darius. He was not removed from it. Nevertheless, God spared His life. Scripture describes what happened in this manner.

At the first light of dawn, the king got up and hurried to the lions' den. When he came near the den, he called to Daniel in an anguished voice, "Daniel, servant of the living God, has your God, whom you serve continually, been able to rescue you from the lions?" Daniel answered, "May the king live forever! My God sent his angel, and he shut the mouths of the lions. They have not hurt me, because I was found innocent in his sight. Nor have I ever done any wrong before you, Your Majesty" (Daniel 6:19-22)

There is no reason why the Lord cannot do the same thing to those who live during the dark period of the great tribulation. Indeed, He is able to shelter Christians during this time.

Thus, we have a number of examples in Scripture of people being protected during times of trouble. Instead of being removed from tribulations and suffering, the Lord supernaturally protected them in the midst of everything.

WHY SHOULD IT BE DIFFERENT IN THE FUTURE?

So here is the issue. If this has been the case with believers from the very beginning, then why should we assume it will be any different for the Christians who are living immediately before the return of Jesus Christ? Why should this last generation of Christians receive any special treatment?

In addition, many who hold this view do not believe that there will even be a unique time of "great tribulation" which will strike the inhabitants of the earth. They contend that the term is symbolic of the sufferings which Christians have also had and will always have.

These are among the reasons given as to why the doctrine of the rapture of the church is rejected by certain Bible-believers.

WHAT DO THE RAPTURE PASSAGES MEAN?

If one rejects the idea that the New Testament speaks of an event known as the rapture of the church then these passages mean something other than what seems to be the obvious meaning. Those who reject the rapture often spiritualize the meaning of the passages. They find a fulfillment that is not literal. Just exactly what these passages do mean is *not* agreed upon by these interpreters.

However, the one thing they do agree upon is that no such event as the rapture of the church will occur.

This sums up the main arguments of those who hold the "no rapture" theory.

SUMMARY TO QUESTION 8
WHY DO SOME BIBLE BELIEVERS CONTEND THAT THERE IS NO SUCH THING AS A RAPTURE? (THE NO RAPTURE THEORY)

There are Christians who reject the idea of a future event where living believers are caught up to meet the Lord in the air; the rapture or translation of the church. Thus, Christians should not look forward to literally experiencing an event known as the rapture. When Paul wrote of this event he did not expect his readers to understand it as something which would literally take place. Neither should we.

There are three basic arguments which are usually advanced in support of this idea. They can be summed up as follows.

First, it is claimed that the English word "rapture" is not found in the Bible. If the word isn't a biblical word, why, it is asked, should we believe in such a doctrine? Thus, it is concluded that rapture is not a biblical word and the doctrine of the rapture is not a biblical doctrine.

Second, Jesus prayed specifically for believers to be kept in this world; not to be taken out. This prayer was not merely for His immediate disciples but also for those who came afterward. Jesus made this clear. Consequently, if Jesus prayed that believers would be kept in the world, then we should not accept the idea that one generation of Christians will be supernaturally taken out in a rapture of the church.

Lastly, the Scripture gives many examples of godly people suffering for their faith. There is no reason to believe it will be any different for those who are living immediately before the Lord returns.

Even if there is a time of Great Tribulation which strikes the earth the Lord can be selective in the way He judges the people as He did in protecting Israel when the plagues of Egypt struck.

As far as what the rapture passages actually mean, there is no consensus of opinion among those who reject the idea of a literal catching up of the true believers in Christ. What they do agree upon is that the rapture or translation of the church will not occur in a literal manner.

These are the main reasons certain Bible-believers reject the idea of the rapture of the church. Consequently, the believers in Jesus need to be prepared for suffering, tribulation, and, in some cases, martyrdom. This will continue until the time the Lord returns to the earth at His Second Coming and sets up His everlasting kingdom.

QUESTION 9

What Are The Biblical Problems
With The "No Rapture" Theory?

The theory that there is no such thing as a rapture of the church, the catching up of living believers to meet the Lord in the air, has gained some followers. Reasons given for this belief include the claim that the word rapture is not found in the Bible, that the doctrine is not taught in Scripture, and that Christians are not promised deliverance from trouble. This view is held by those who are Bible-believers.

However, there are other Bible-believing Christians who reject this idea. There are a number of reasons as to why this is so. We can summarize them in the following way.

1. THE WORD RAPTURE IS FOUND IN THE BIBLE

To begin with, the word rapture is indeed found in the Bible; it is in the Latin Bible! The English word rapture is taken from the Latin word *rapere* which means "to catch away" or "to snatch away." It is a translation of the Greek word *harpadzo* which basically has the same meaning. Therefore, it is wrong to say that the word rapture is not found in Scripture. It is. It is simply not found in the English Bible.

Furthermore, the phrase "Second Coming" is not found in the English Bible either. Yet nobody wants to argue that the Bible does not teach the Second Coming of Jesus Christ! Moreover, neither do we find the phrases "the seventieth week of Daniel," "pre-millennial," or the "tribulation period" in Scripture. Again, while the exact wording or the specific phrases may not be found in Scripture this is not the real issue. The issue is this: does the Bible teach these truths? That's the question which must be answered.

THE DOCTRINE OF THE RAPTURE IS TAUGHT IN SCRIPTURE

This brings us to the real issue which must be addressed. The doctrine of the rapture, or the catching up of believers in Christ, is clearly taught in the New Testament. Whether one wants to call this event: "the rapture" "the gathering of believers" the "great catching away" the "translation of believers" or something similar, the doctrine is certainly taught in the New Testament. Two passages explain this event in great detail. They are as follows.

1 THESSALONIANS 4:13-18

Paul wrote to the Thessalonian church about the catching up of the church to meet the Lord. He put it this way.

> Brothers and sisters, we do not want you to be uninformed about those who sleep in death, so that you do not grieve like the rest, who have no hope For we believe that Jesus died and rose again, and so we believe that God will bring with Jesus those who have fallen asleep in him. According to the Lord's word, we tell you that we who are still alive, who are left until the coming of the Lord, will certainly not precede those who have fallen asleep. For the Lord himself will come down from heaven, with a loud command, with the voice of the archangel and with the trumpet call of God, and the dead in Christ will rise first. After that, we who are still alive and are left will be caught up together with them in the clouds to meet the Lord in the air. And so we will be with the Lord forever. Therefore encourage one another with these words (1 Thessalonians 4:13-18).

Here we have a clear description of this coming event. Unless we assume these words need to be spiritualized or understood in an allegorical manner, we are forced to accept the idea that this is speaking of an actual future event.

1 CORINTHIANS 15:50-55

In addition, we find another passage written to a different church where the same truth is taught. Paul also wrote to the Corinthians about this wonderful event. He stated in very clear terms that not all believers would die but rather some would be instantaneously changed.

> I declare to you, brothers and sisters, that flesh and blood cannot inherit the kingdom of God, nor does the perishable inherit the imperishable. Listen, I tell you a mystery: We will not all sleep, but we will all be changed--in a flash, in the twinkling of an eye, at the last trumpet. For the trumpet will sound, the dead will be raised imperishable, and we will be changed. For the perishable must clothe itself with the imperishable, and the mortal with immortality. When the perishable has been clothed with the imperishable, and the mortal with immortality, then the saying that is written will come true: Death has been swallowed up in victory. Where, O death, is your victory? Where, O death, is your sting? (1 Corinthians 15:50-55)

These passages speak for themselves. As we have already noted, there are at least fourteen things we learn about this doctrine from the teaching of Scripture. There is no doubt that Scripture speaks of a time when living believers will be caught up to meet the Lord in the air. The main question that is in doubt concerns the timing of the rapture. In other words, the issue is not *if* it will happen, the issue is *when* it will take place.

3. JESUS' PRAYER FOR HIS DISCIPLES DOES NOT ANSWER THIS QUESTION

While it is true that Jesus prayed that His disciples, as well as those who followed them, would not be taken out of the world, this does not deal with the specific issue of the rapture. As a general rule, Christians do suffer because we live in a sinful world. This, however, does not mean that there may not be an exception to this general principle. Therefore, this one statement of Jesus should be interpreted in light of everything which is taught on this subject.

4. THE GREAT TRIBULATION IS A UNIQUE PERIOD OF TIME IN HISTORY

This brings us to our next point. Nobody denies that godly people have suffered from the beginning of time and that they continue to suffer. Many times they suffer unjustly. Furthermore, it is admitted that the Lord is able to protect His own in the midst of difficulties or in the midst of His own judgments. This is not in question.

However, the issue is not whether Christians will have problems and tribulations, the issue is whether or not Christians will be upon the earth during an unprecedented time of trouble; the great tribulation.

Indeed, Jesus said the following about this time.

> For then there will be great distress, unequaled from the beginning of the world until now--and never to be equaled again. (Matthew 24:21

Consequently, this period of time will be unique in the history of the world because God will pour out His divine wrath upon the inhabitants of the earth. As the Lord stated, it will be a period like no other which the world has ever experienced. Furthermore, we also read that God has NOT appointed His people to suffer His wrath.

> For God did not appoint us to suffer wrath but to receive salvation through our Lord Jesus Christ. (1 Thessalonians 5:9)

Since the great tribulation period is a time of His wrath the idea of the Lord removing believers before this time period is consistent with who He is and how He deals with believers.

Therefore, all passages which speak of Christians suffering or going through times of trouble are irrelevant to this question. The issue is simple: will God allow His people to remain on the earth when He Himself sends the massive judgments the Scripture records? What does Scripture specifically say about Christians and this unique time period? This is the *only* question that matters.

When all the evidence is considered we must conclude that the rapture of the church is indeed a biblical doctrine. Many specific details are given to us about what will occur.

Consequently, if there is such a coming event as the catching away of the living believers we should attempt to discover from Scripture exactly when this is going to occur as well as how we should prepare for it. And the answer as to how we should prepare for it is simple; believe in Jesus Christ!

SUMMARY TO QUESTION 9
WHAT ARE THE BIBLICAL PROBLEMS WITH THE NO RAPTURE THEORY?

The doctrine of the rapture, or translation, of the church while seemingly is clearly taught in the New Testament is actually denied by some devout Christians. They contend the Bible does not teach that such an event will occur.

Those who hold this view usually argue that since the word rapture is not found in the Bible the doctrine is not biblical. Furthermore, they cite Jesus' prayer which He made on the night of His betrayal. He prayed that believers would be kept in the world not taken out from it. This means it is not God's desire that His people be removed from the troubles in this world. Finally, they point out that from the beginning of time, godly men and women have suffered great persecution and martyrdom. Thus, there is no reason to assume that certain ones will be removed from a future time of trouble.

These objections are without merit. First, the word rapture is found in the Bible; in the Latin translation of First Thessalonians 4:17. Thus, the term is found in Scripture. While the precise term "rapture" may not be found in English translations neither do we find the phrase "Second Coming" in Scripture. Nobody wants to deny that the Scriptures do not teach the return of Christ merely because this exact phrase is not found in the Bible. We could say the same thing about phrases such as "the Tribulation Period" "Pre-millennial" and "The Seventieth Week of Daniel." People do not reject the teachings about these subjects merely because the specific phrase is lacking in Scripture. The issue is not the phrase used; rather it is, "What does the Bible have to say about this subject?"

There is something else that needs to be considered. There is much more to the doctrine of the rapture than the mere term appearing in Scripture. Indeed, the doctrine is clearly taught in the Bible. Two passages, 1 Thessalonians 4:13-18 and 1 Corinthians 15:50-58, give many specific details of this coming event. There is no reason whatsoever to understand these verses in anything but a literal, straightforward manner. Other passages also make reference to this coming event.

The fact that Jesus prayed that His followers would be kept in the world, and not taken out, does not solve the problem. Since the Great Tribulation is an unprecedented time of trouble, when the wrath of God comes upon the people of the earth, there is every reason to believe that the Lord would remove His people from this time period.

Thus, the fact that the Lord generally allows His people to suffer trials and tribulations does not mean that He cannot remove them if He so desires. Indeed, this is the issue in question. We cannot, and should not, rule out the possibility of this occurring because Scripture does not rule it out. Therefore, these words of Jesus do not directly apply to this question.

Furthermore, the nature of the Great Tribulation constitutes a solid reason as to why the New Testament believers would be removed. It is a time when God's wrath is poured out on the people of the world. It is a time of judgment for unbelief and rejection of Him. Finally, Scripture specifically says that the Lord has not appointed His people to His wrath but rather to deliverance through Jesus Christ.

Therefore, it is clear that the rapture of the church is a biblical doctrine. At some time in the future, known only to the Lord, Jesus will descend from heaven, resurrect the dead believers "in Christ" and instantly change the bodies of believers who are living while catching them up to meet Him in the air. This is our blessed hope. Such a hope should not be minimized or denied.

QUESTION 10

Why Do Some People Believe That Not All Christians Will Be Raptured? (The Partial Rapture Theory)

Most Bible-believers, who believe in a future rapture, contend that *all* true Christians will be taken in the "catching up" of the church, to meet the Lord. This is true no matter if one believes in a Pre-Tribulation, Mid-Tribulation, a Pre-Wrath or a Post-Tribulation rapture.

However, there are exceptions to this. Indeed, there are Bible students who teach that only those believers who are faithful or spiritual will be raptured when Jesus snatches away His church unto Himself. In other words, going up to meet the Lord in the rapture is conditioned upon our obedience, our spirituality. This idea is known as the "partial rapture" theory.

THE THEORY EXPLAINED

Those who hold to the partial rapture are generally in agreement on a number of things. First they believe the rapture will take place before the great tribulation period. In this sense they hold to a Pre-Tribulation rapture.

However, when this event occurs, it will be only the worthy, or spiritual, believers which are taken up to meet the Lord. Those who are not worthy will be left behind to face the great tribulation period. All of those who accept the partial rapture theory agree on this.

THERE IS NO AGREEMENT AS TO WHAT WILL HAPPEN TO THE ONES LEFT BEHIND

Yet, there is no agreement among the partial rapturists as to what will happen to those Christians who are not taken up to meet the Lord. Some think they will have to endure the sufferings of the great tribulation period in its entirety. It is taught that the great tribulation will purify these carnal Christians before they enter heaven. Therefore, it is like a purgatory.

Others think that there will be a series of raptures. The first rapture occurs before the great tribulation period. Then there will be other times during the great tribulation when groups of believers are taken up to meet the Lord. In other words, the rapture is not merely a one-off event.

Support for the partial rapture is usually stated as follows.

BELIEVERS MUST BE SPIRITUALLY WORTHY TO MEET THE LORD

Those who advocate a partial rapture reckon that the catching away of believers must either be by God's grace or as a reward for our faithfulness. They think the Bible teaches that it will be based upon our works. In other words, being caught up in the rapture will be a reward for our faithful service to Christ.

This being the case, it is asked, "Why should the Lord translate carnal or unspiritual believers into His presence?" Those living in a state of sin do not deserve to be taken up in the rapture. Consequently, they will be left behind.

In support of this position, they note the numerous exhortations in the Bible where believers are to watch, to be faithful, to be ready for Christ's coming, and to live Spirit-filled lives. Partial rapturists see these exhortations as teaching that the rapture of the church is a reward for faithfulness. In other words, it is earned by the way in which we behave. We must be obedient.

THE EXAMPLE OF ENOCH

Further evidence is found in the life of the patriarch Enoch. He was translated into heaven because he lived a godly life. Scripture says the following about what happened to him.

> Enoch walked with God, and he was not, for God took him (Genesis 5:24).

The obedience of Enoch is what allowed him to be "taken up" or raptured. In a similar manner, those Christians who are alive at the time of the rapture of the church will be caught up to meet the Lord if they are living an obedient life. Otherwise they will be left behind.

THERE IS A PROMISE OF REWARDS TO THE OVERCOMERS

This line of argumentation is supported by Scripture. In the Lord's letters to the seven churches of Revelation we find a repetition of the phrase "to him that overcomes" or "to those who are victorious." For example, the Lord said the following to the church at Pergamum.

> Whoever has ears, let them hear what the Spirit says to the churches. To those who are victorious, I will give some of the hidden manna. I will also give each of them a white stone with a new name written on it, known only to the one who receives it (Revelation 2:17).

This has been understood to mean that those who have become spiritually strong and mature enough will be spared the horrendous suffering of the great tribulation. Thus, Scripture itself divides believers into two groups "overcomers" and "non-overcomers" or the "victorious ones" and the "non-victorious ones."

3. THE PARABLE OF THE TEN VIRGINS OR MAIDENS ILLUSTRATES THAT SOME BELIEVERS WILL BE LEFT BEHIND

The story of Jesus about the ten maidens, or virgins, is used as an illustration of certain believers being left behind. We read the following.

> At that time the kingdom of heaven will be like ten virgins who took their lamps and went out to meet the bridegroom. Five of them were foolish and five were wise. . . . But while they were on their way to buy the oil, the bridegroom arrived. The virgins who were ready went in with him to the wedding banquet. And the door was shut. Later the others also came, 'Lord, Lord,' they said, 'open the door for us!' But he replied, 'Truly I tell you, I don't know you.' Therefore keep watch, because you do not know the day or the hour (Matthew 25:1-2, 10-13).

In this story, we are told of people who were not ready for the appearance of the groom; a reference to Jesus. In the same manner, there will be believers who are not ready for the coming of the Lord. Like those in Jesus' story, these Christians will be left behind.

4. THERE ARE MANY WARNING PASSAGES ABOUT THE LORD'S COMING

The Bible is also filled with passages which warn believers about the coming of the Lord. For example, Jesus said.

> Be careful, or your hearts will be weighed down with carousing, drunkenness and the anxieties of life, and that day will close on you suddenly like a trap. For it will come on all those who live on the face of the whole earth. Be always on the watch, and pray that you may be able to escape all that is about to happen, and that you may be able to stand before the Son of Man (Luke 21:34-36).

We are to be watchful and ready. Indeed Jesus emphasized that believers are to live godly lives in order to *escape* the coming events

In another place, we read of Jesus stressing the need for Christians to be alert. He said.

> It will be good for those servants whose master finds them watching when he comes. Truly I tell you, he will dress

himself to serve, will have them recline at the table and will come and wait on them. It will be good for those servants whose master finds them ready, even if he comes in the middle of the night or toward daybreak (Luke 12:37-38).

Here Jesus contrasts the believers who are watching and are blessed with those who are not watching and will miss out on the blessings. In fact, some who hold to the partial rapture divide the church into two parts; the victorious church and the slumbering church.

THESE WARNINGS MUST HAVE SOME MEANING

It is argued that these warnings must mean something. To those who believe in a partial rapture, these warnings are given so that Christians will be prepared for the rapture; prepared so that they do not miss it.

SOME BELIEVERS WILL BE ASHAMED AT JESUS' COMING

Furthermore, the Scripture says that there will be certain believers who will actually be ashamed at the time of Jesus' coming. John wrote the following.

And now, dear children, continue in him, so that when he appears we may be confident and unashamed before him at his coming (1 John 2:28).

To some, this indicates that immature or unspiritual believers will not be taken with the godly believers when the rapture of the church occurs. Instead they will be ashamed because they are left behind to experience the great tribulation.

In addition, there seems to be a specific test for those who will be raptured. We read about it in Hebrews.

So Christ was sacrificed once to take away the sins of many; and he will appear a second time, not to bear sin, but to bring salvation to those who are waiting for him (Hebrews 9:28).

According to this passage, the rapture of the church will only include those who are *eagerly* awaiting His coming. Obviously, this does not refer to every Christian.

6. GODLY INTERPRETERS HAVE HELD THIS VIEW

The belief that the rapture of the church is not a work of grace but something based upon our obedience has convinced some Bible teachers that not every Christian will be taken up when the rapture of the church occurs. In fact, a number of well-respected and godly interpreters have held and promoted this position. They insist that only those who are watching and waiting for the Lord's return will meet Him at the rapture.

Therefore, if a believer in Jesus Christ desires to be a participant in the rapture of the church he or she must remain obedient to the Lord. Otherwise they will be left behind.

SUMMARY TO QUESTION 10
WHY DO SOME PEOPLE BELIEVE THAT NOT ALL CHRISTIANS WILL BE RAPTURED? (THE PARTIAL RAPTURE THEORY)

The partial rapture theory believes and teaches the rapture of the church will occur at some time in the future. It also says that it will happen before the seven-year seventieth week of Daniel, the last seven years before Christ returns. This is also known the Great Tribulation period. In this sense, the partial rapture theory is pre-tribulational in their belief.

Yet this theory argues that not everyone who has placed their faith in Jesus Christ will be raptured before the Great Tribulation occurs. Some believers will be left behind. There will be certain Christians who will not be ready when the Lord first comes for His church. The spiritual mature will be ready; the spiritual immature will not and hence will not be taken to meet the Lord in the air.

There are differences of opinion as to what will happen to those believers who will be left behind. Some believe that they will have to endure the entire period of the Great Tribulation. Others think that these left-behind believers will be raptured in groups during these final seven years before Jesus returns.

Those who believe in a partial rapture assert that the rapture will be based either upon God's grace alone or by our own worthiness. They think there are a number of passages which teach that the rapture is a reward for the faithful service of believers. It is not guaranteed to everyone who believes in Jesus. They insist the Bible teaches that Christians must be worthy to meet the Lord. Those "unworthy" cannot be assured they will be taken up in the rapture. Enoch is an example of a believer who was taken up to meet the Lord because he was "worthy." Living believers, like Enoch, must behave in a worthy manner to be included in the rapture.

Numerous other Scriptures are cited for support. For example, the Book of Revelation divides believers into two categories; the overcomers and the non-overcomers. Those who overcome will be taken up to meet the Lord in the air while the non-overcomers will be left behind.

QUESTION 11

What Are The Biblical Problems With The Partial Rapture Theory?

The partial rapture theory holds that the rapture of the church occurs before the great tribulation period. However, it also claims that not every believer in Jesus Christ will be taken to meet the Lord at that time. It is contended that only those which are spiritually mature will be gathered together with Him in the clouds. Those who are carnal Christians will be left behind.

While there have been godly people who have held this theory there are many biblical objections to it. We can list them as follows.

1. THERE ARE NO VERSES WHICH TEACH A PARTIAL RAPTURE

To begin with, there are no verses which teach the doctrine of a "partial rapture." None whatsoever! In fact, just the opposite is true. Every passage which speaks of the rapture assumes that *all* believers, no matter their spiritual state, will be taken up.

THE RAPTURE IS BASED UPON GRACE, NOT WORKS

The rapture of the church is based upon God's grace, not upon our own works. Paul said those who are "in Christ" will be raptured. This includes all believers. Indeed, by definition, one who believes in Jesus is "in Christ." This is very important to understand.

3. A PURGATORY ON EARTH IS CREATED FOR THOSE LEFT BEHIND

In addition, the partial rapture idea creates a type of purgatory for the spiritually immature believers. They would have to suffer through the greatest period of judgment the world has ever seen. While many would die, *all* would suffer. This type of suffering is contrary to the teaching of Scripture about the grace of God. Jesus Christ paid for all of our sins; we do not have to have them purged from us.

PASSAGES USED TO ARGUE FOR A PARTIAL RAPTURE ARE MISAPPLIED

The passages which are used to establish a partial rapture are misapplied. In most cases they are not dealing with true believers but rather with people who only profess to believe.

For example, the parable of the ten virgins does not teach that some Christians are left behind. To the contrary, those who tried to get into the wedding feast were told by the Lord "I never knew you." This speaks of unbelievers, not believers.

SHOULD WE ALSO EXPECT A PARTIAL RESURRECTION?

There is another point to consider. If the partial rapture position is correct, and if only the mature believers are taken to meet the Lord, then it logically follows that the same basis of selection would have to be applied to those Christians who have died. This would mean that only those who died in a state of spiritual maturity would be resurrected at that time. The others would remain in their graves. Exactly when these carnal Christians would be raised from the dead is not recorded in Scripture.

However, Paul does not limit the resurrection to only those who died in a state of spiritual maturity. To the contrary, he says "all" will be raised. This means the spiritual as well as the less spiritual Christians.

6. BELIEVERS ARE NOT DIVIDED INTO OVERCOMERS AND NON-OVERCOMERS FOR THE RAPTURE

The idea that believers are divided into two groups for purposes of the rapture, the overcomers and non-overcomers, is not biblical. Indeed, of all the churches which Paul addressed there was none more spiritually immature than the Corinthians. In fact, he began his letter to them in the following way.

> I appeal to you, brothers and sisters, in the name of our Lord Jesus Christ, that all of you agree with one another in what you say and that there be no divisions among you, but that you be perfectly united in mind and thought. My brothers and sisters, some from Chloe's household have informed me that there are quarrels among you (1 Corinthians 1:10-11).

The Corinthian church was made up of spiritually immature Christians. Yet when Paul wrote to this carnal group of believers he told them that *all* of them would be changed. He said.

> Listen, I tell you a mystery: We will not all sleep, but we will all be changed (1 Corinthians 15:51).

Paul did not make a distinction between the spiritually mature Christians and the carnal Christians with respect to the rapture of the church. Instead the apostle stated that all will be taken.

It must be noted that those which hold to the partial-rapture theory correctly stress the idea of godly living. Indeed, John tells us that the expectation of Christ's return is a purifying hope.

> All who have this hope in him purify themselves, just as he is pure (1 John 3:3).

However, this does not mean we should make the participation in the rapture dependent upon our holy living. Scripture does not do this and neither should we.

7. THERE IS NO TIME FOR THE JUDGMENT SEAT OF CHRIST TO OCCUR

Paul wrote that *all* believers are to appear before the judgment seat of Christ. He wrote.

> For we must all appear before the judgment seat of Christ, that everyone may receive what is due them for the things done while in the body, whether good or bad (2 Corinthians 5:10).

Since all believers are supposed to appear before Jesus Christ to receive their rewards, if some were left behind at the rapture, or not raised from the dead, then it seems to follow that there must be another time of judgment for them. When would that judgment occur? The Bible gives no indication of such a judgment taking place.

THE PARTIAL RAPTURE THEORY MAY LEAD TO SPIRITUAL PRIDE

There is also the possibility that the partial rapture theory may lead to a certain spiritual arrogance, or pride, on behalf of those who embrace it. Those who hold this doctrine often assume that *they* are among the group which will be translated into heaven. Thus, they see themselves as in a different spiritual category when compared to other believers. This is not something which Scripture encourages believers to do. We are all sinners who are saved by God's grace and we are still sinners who are kept by God's grace.

HOW DOES ONE KNOW WHEN THEY ARE SPIRITUALLY MATURE?

One crucial question for those who hold the partial rapture theory is this: how does one know they have reached the point of readiness to be included in the rapture? What does it take for a believer to be assured that he or she will be taken up to meet the Lord? What are the requirements?

Obviously this question cannot be given a specific answer because there is no answer. Nobody on this earth can determine exactly how to define a spiritually mature person. Therefore, it is meaningless to attempt to make the distinction.

CONCLUSION: THE RAPTURE OF THE CHURCH IS NOT PARTIAL

Though many godly people, with seemingly the best of motives, have held to the partial rapture doctrine, we find there are a number of serious problems with it that make it difficult, if not impossible, to accept. When the Lord Jesus comes to rapture, or snatch away, His people to Himself, the church, His body, will be complete. Indeed, no parts of the body of Christ will be missing. Therefore, at the time of the rapture no true believer in Jesus Christ will be left behind.

Therefore, the question we still face is this: when will the rapture occur with respect to the seventieth week of Daniel? Will it be before, sometime during, or at the end of this future seven-year period?

SUMMARY TO QUESTION 11
WHAT ARE THE BIBLICAL PROBLEMS WITH THE PARTIAL RAPTURE THEORY?

The partial rapture theory says that the rapture of the church will be pre-tribulational or before the Great Tribulation period; seven years before Jesus Christ returns to the earth. However, this theory says that not every Christian will be caught up to meet the Lord in the air at that time. It is only those Christians who are walking worthy, the ones who are spiritually mature, that will be raptured.

Though this view has been held by some very good Bible teachers, it has never gained much popularity. To begin with, there are no verses whatsoever which teach a partial rapture. None. The partial rapture view has to be read into the text. The evidence is just not there.

Furthermore, not only do we find no passages teaching a partial rapture, we find the opposite to be the case! The plain teaching of the Bible concerning the rapture of the church is that "all" true believers will be taken up to meet the Lord when this event occurs. This is taught over and over again in Scripture.

In addition, the partial rapture view is based upon the idea that participating in the rapture is because of our works rather than God's grace. According to this position, participating in the rapture of the church is something a believer earns; it is not bestowed by Jesus Christ through His grace. It is seen as a reward. This is contrary to the totality of the teaching of Scripture on the subject of salvation; it is certainly not something we can earn.

Furthermore, a partial rapture creates a type of earthly purgatory for those left behind. Believers in Christ are purged of their sins until they are made ready to meet the Lord. However, this is completely contradictory to the biblical teaching that salvation is by grace alone. We don't save ourselves; we do not keep ourselves saved.

The passages which are cited for a partial rapture are misapplied. For example, the five foolish maidens in Jesus' parable are not believers. Jesus said to them, "I never knew you." They were never His.

Passages which warn believers to be ready for the coming of the Lord are not given to warn believers that certain unspiritual Christians will be left behind. Rather they are given as encouragement for us to live godly lives in anticipation of His return.

The Apostle Paul says all deceased believers are to be raised from the dead. However, if the partial rapture view is correct, then certain ones would not be raised at the time of the rapture; unless we assume every believer who has died in the past has died in a state of spiritual maturity. Undoubtedly nobody wants to insist upon that! While the Bible says that the church is one body the partial rapture view wrongly divides the body of Christ into diverse groups based upon their spiritual level. There is no biblical justification whatsoever for dividing the unity of body of Christ into various levels of spirituality.

Furthermore, Paul said all believers are to appear before the judgment seat of Christ to receive rewards. When will this occur? If the partial rapture theory is correct, then the judgment seat would have to wait until after Christ returns to earth. This is difficult to reconcile with what the Bible teaches on the subject. There is also the pride factor to be considered. Those who assume they will be the spiritual ones caught up in the rapture could be overtaken with pride.

One last question concerns how to determine who is worthy and who is not. How do any of us know? What are the criteria? Since the Bible does not give us any specific standard nobody could know, from one moment to the next, if they can be considered spiritually mature to the place where they would be taken up in the rapture of the church. While the partial rapture view has been accepted by some Bible-believing Christians, no major Christian group has ever embraced this position.

QUESTION 12

What Is The Mid-Tribulation Rapture View?

While most Bible-believing Christians, who believe in a future rapture, embrace either a Post-Tribulation or Pre-Tribulation view with respect to its timing there is a minority which accepts neither. Instead they believe that the best understanding of this coming event is to place it at the mid-point of the final seven years before Jesus Christ returns. This is usually known as the Mid-Tribulation rapture view.

It should be noted that those who hold this view usually do not use the term "Mid-Tribulation rapturists" to describe themselves. Rather many prefer to classify themselves as holding to Pretribulationism.

The reason for this is that they believe Jesus Christ is coming before the "great tribulation" which they believe occurs during the *last* half of the seventieth week of Daniel. Thus, while Pre-Tribulationists believe the tribulation lasts seven years the Mid-Tribulationists think that it lasts only three and one half years.

We can explain this view as follows.

THE SEVENTIETH WEEK OF DANIEL IS STILL FUTURE

Those which hold this perspective of the timing of the rapture accept some of the arguments of Pre-Tribulationism as well as some of the arguments for Post-Tribulationism. For one thing, they believe that the seventieth week of Daniel is future. We read the following words in Daniel.

> He will confirm a covenant with many for one 'seven.' In the middle of the 'seven' he will put an end to sacrifice and offering. And at the temple he will set up an abomination that causes desolation, until the end that is decreed is poured out on him (Daniel 9:27).

Thus, Mid-Tribulationism, like Pre-Tribulationism, and many Post-Tribulationists believe this seventieth week is still future.

2. THERE IS A THREE AND ONE HALF YEAR INTERVAL BETWEEN THE RAPTURE AND THE SECOND COMING

Like the Pre-Tribulation position, those which hold the Mid-Tribulation theory believe there is an interval of time between the rapture of the church and the Second Coming of Jesus Christ. This is opposed to the Post-Tribulation view which sees no interval. The difference between the Pre-Tribulation and the Mid-Tribulation view is the *length* of the interval. Mid-Tribulationism has a three and one half year interval while the Pre-Trib view has seven years.

3. THE CHURCH IS FOUND IN THE OLD TESTAMENT

Contrary to the Pre-Tribulation view, those who hold the Mid-Tribulation position believe the church is found in the Old Testament. They see the first half of the seventieth week of Daniel as referring to the church.

Furthermore, they believe God's program with respect to Israel and the church are not kept entirely separate. Instead they overlap. The church will participate in the first half of Daniel's seventieth week but will not be around when the most severe judgment occurs. This last half of the seven years is known as the time of "Jacob's trouble" and deals with the nation Israel.

4. THE CHURCH IS FOUND IN JESUS' OLIVET DISCOURSE

The Olivet Discourse records the teaching of Jesus regarding coming events. It is recorded in detail in Matthew 24 and 25. These chapters are regarded by Mid-Tribulationists as directed to the New Testament church and not merely to a future time for Israel. The apostles are seen as representative of the church and therefore, the rapture of the church is included in these words of Jesus. As already stated, while God does have distinct programs for Israel and the church, there is some overlap in these programs. We find this overlap in the Olivet Discourse.

5. THE GREAT TRIBULATION LASTS THREE AND ONE HALF YEARS

This brings us to one of the differences between the Pre-Tribulation view and Mid-Tribulation view. Mid-Tribulationism emphasizes that the New Testament church has been promised that they will experience persecution and tribulation. Thus, since all who live godly in Christ Jesus will experience such things, the sufferings of the church in the first half of the seventieth week of Daniel fits with the calling of the church.

Consequently, the first three and one half years of the final seven year period will find the church on the earth suffering persecution and in many cases, martyrdom. This, however, is the wrath of *humans*, not the wrath God. The divine wrath, the great tribulation, does not begin until the midpoint of the last seven year period.

Thus, the Mid-Tribulation view does not see the opening of the seals, as recorded in Revelation chapter six, and the various trumpet judgments which follow, as signs of God's divine wrath. Indeed, they do not believe the wrath occurs until the *last* of the seven trumpets sounds. The church will be raptured *before* this divine wrath is unleashed.

6. THE SEVENTH TRUMPET OR LAST TRUMPET SIGNALS THE RAPTURE

According to the Mid-Tribulation view, the great tribulation begins with the seventh trumpet in the Book of Revelation. Scripture says.

The seventh angel sounded his trumpet, and there were loud voices in heaven, which said: "The kingdom of the world has become the kingdom of our Lord and of his Messiah, and he will reign for ever and ever" (Revelation 11:15).

The seventh trumpet is blown in the middle of the seventieth week of Daniel. This begins the last half of the final seven year period in which unprecedented judgments take place. The outpouring of the wrath of God is described in detail in Revelation 16-18.

The seventh trumpet is also equated with the last trumpet which Paul speaks of in First Corinthians 15:52 and First Thessalonians 4:16. We read the following in First Corinthians.

In a flash, in the twinkling of an eye, at the last trumpet. For the trumpet will sound, the dead will be raised imperishable, and we will be changed (1 Corinthians 15:52).

This trumpet sounds the call to believers to meet Jesus Christ in the air; the rapture.

Therefore, the rapture of the church occurs during the midpoint of the final seven years. This is three and one half years before the Second Coming of Jesus Christ and before the wrath of God is poured out upon the inhabitants of the earth.

7. THE SNATCHING UP OF THE TWO WITNESSES IN REVELATION 11 SYMBOLIZES THE RAPTURE

Many who hold the Mid-Tribulation position also believe that the two witnesses described in the Book of Revelation represent the church. They are caught away, or raptured at this time. We read.

But after the three and a half days the breath of life from God entered them, and they stood on their feet, and terror struck those who saw them. Then they heard a loud voice from heaven saying to them, "Come up here." And they went up to heaven in a cloud, while their enemies looked on (Revelation 11:11,12)

The three and one half days are thought to symbolize the first three and one half years of the seventieth week of Daniel. The two witnesses are said to symbolize the believers in Jesus Christ. At that time they are taken up to meet the Lord; the rapture of the church.

8. THERE IS NO IMMINENT COMING OF CHRIST

Since the rapture does not occur until three and one half years into the seventieth week of Daniel, or great tribulation period, there is no such thing as an imminent coming of Christ.

In other words, a number of events must necessarily happen before the rapture of the church occurs. Consequently, believers cannot look for this event to take place at "any moment." Indeed, there are several biblical predictions which must be fulfilled before Christ can come back for His bride, the church.

This sums up the basic arguments which are put forth by those who see the rapture occurring three and one half years into the seventieth week of Daniel. As we have indicated, it is a minority position held by Bible-believing Christians.

SUMMARY TO QUESTION 12
WHAT IS THE MID-TRIBULATION RAPTURE VIEW?

The mid-tribulation rapture position is similar to the pre-tribulation viewpoint in that it holds that believers will not have to experience the wrath of God. The church will be taken out of the world before God's dreadful judgments come upon the earth. Like the pre-tribulation view, it is believed that there will be an interval between the time the Lord removes His church from the earth and when He comes again in judgment. The issue at hand is the amount of time. Those who hold the pre-tribulational position say seven years while those who hold the mid-tribulational position say three years and one half years.

Because they believe the Great Tribulation does not begin until the last three and one half years of Daniel's seventieth week, those holding this view do not usually like to call themselves mid-tribulationists. They are pre-tribulationists in the sense that they see the Great Tribulation as lasting only three and one half years. However, for convenience sake, we should label this view the mid-tribulation rapture position.

The mid-tribulation view sees the seventieth week of Daniel, or the tribulation period, divided into two distinct three and one half year segments. The first three and one half years is the wrath of humanity against the church while the second three and one half years is the wrath of God against the human race.

According to Paul, the rapture of the church takes place at the "last trump." This trumpet blast is identified with the seventh trumpet of Revelation 11:15 by those who hold the mid-tribulation rapture position. This occurs in the middle of Daniel's seventieth week.

Thus, those who hold this position deny the doctrine of imminency; that Jesus Christ could come back to the world at any time. There is at least a three and one half year period before Christ can return for the true believers in Him.

This view says that the church is not a mystery which was unknown until the New Testament times. It sees the church as the main focus of the first half of the seventieth week of Daniel as recorded in Daniel 9. The last three and one half years, when the severe judgments occur, is the time of Jacob's trouble. It is the time Israel is again in the spotlight with the New Testament church removed from the world by means of the rapture.

While the Lord has a distinct program for the nation Israel as well as one for the New Testament church, these programs overlap according to the mid-tribulation rapture view.

In addition, those who hold the mid-tribulation view believe that Jesus spoke of such things in His Olivet Discourse. They believe those words were directed to the church; not mainly to the people of Israel.

All in all, those who hold the mid-tribulation position believe their understanding of the timing of the rapture solves the problems found in both the pre-tribulation view and post-tribulation view.

What Are Some Of The Biblical Problems With The Mid-Tribulation Rapture Position?

The Mid-Tribulation rapture view is the theory that the rapture of the church occurs three and one half years before Jesus Christ comes again to the earth. Like the Pre-Tribulational rapture, this view says there is an interval of time between the rapture of the church and the Second Coming of Christ.

However, unlike the Pre-Tribulation position it says the great tribulation is only three and one half years in length. According to this theory, the rapture occurs immediately before this period of God's wrath. Those who hold this position think it provides better answers to the rapture question than does the Pre-Tribulation or Post-Tribulation viewpoint.

OBJECTIONS TO MID-TRIB FROM THE PRE-TRIB PERSPECTIVE

The following are the main objections against the Mid-Tribulation rapture perspective from those who hold the Pre-Tribulation view.

THE CHURCH IS A MYSTERY IN THE OLD TESTAMENT

Contrary to the Mid-Tribulation position, the church is not found in the Old Testament. It is a mystery, or sacred secret, which was not revealed until the New Testament period. Paul made this clear.

> I have become its servant by the commission God gave me
> to present to you the word of God in its fullness-the mystery

that has been kept hidden for ages and generations, but is now disclosed to the Lord's people. To them God has chosen to make known among the Gentiles the glorious riches of this mystery, which is Christ in you, the hope of glory (Colossians 1:25-27)

Therefore, we should not look for the church in the Old Testament.

2. THE ENTIRE SEVENTY WEEKS OF DANIEL ONLY HAS TO DO WITH ISRAEL

Furthermore, Daniel was told that the entire period of the "seventy sevens" was explicitly decreed for "his people," the Jews.

Seventy 'sevens' are decreed for your people and your holy city to finish transgression, to put an end to sin, to atone for wickedness, to bring in everlasting righteousness, to seal up vision and prophecy and to anoint the Most Holy Place (Daniel 9:24).

The programs for the nation Israel and the church do not overlap as the Mid-Tribulation rapture position states. God does not begin the last seven year period of His dealings with Israel until the New Testament church, made up of Jews and Gentiles, is removed from the world by means of the rapture. Indeed, we never find in Scripture where God is using both Israel and the New Testament church at the same time as His divine agents.

3. THE OLIVET DISCOURSE IS DIRECTED AT ISRAEL

The Pre-Tribulation position is that the Olivet Discourse is *primarily* aimed at the nation Israel. The questions by the disciples, and the answers given by Jesus, are in a Jewish context. Indeed, the questions which were asked concern the destruction of Jerusalem, the Temple and the coming of the Lord. It is, therefore, a mistake to assume that Jesus' answers are directed at the New Testament church.

4. THERE IS NO REASON TO BELIEVE THE GREAT TRIBULATION BEGINS WITH THE SEVENTH TRUMPET

One of the main objections is equating the beginning of the great tribulation with the sounding of the seventh trumpet in the Book of Revelation. Those which hold the Pre-Tribulation rapture perspective see no reason to think the rapture of the church, and the great tribulation, occur here. Instead, they see the entire seven year period as a time of God's wrath; not merely the last three and one half years.

Furthermore, these trumpets in the Book of Revelation are trumpets of *judgment* while the trumpet associated with the rapture of the church is a trumpet of *deliverance* from the curse of this earth. The trumpets in Revelation announce God's wrath is coming while the trumpet that sounds at the rapture calls the believers to come away and be with their Lord. These are not the same trumpet blasts!

5. THE TWO WITNESSES ARE NOT SYMBOLIC OF THE CHURCH

The two witnesses in the Book of Revelation should be viewed as two human beings living at the time of the end. Indeed, they are called prophets, their unique clothing is described for us, and we are told of the specific plagues they send to those upon the earth.

Furthermore, it is stated that they are killed and that their dead bodies lie for three days in the streets of Jerusalem, a literal city. Then, after three days, these prophets are raised back to life. This is clearly describing two literal people who will be alive at that time. It is not symbolic of the New Testament church and the rapture.

6. THE DOCTRINE OF IMMINENCY IS TAUGHT IN SCRIPTURE

The Mid-Tribulation position denies that the coming of Christ could be at any moment. This agrees with the Post-Tribulation viewpoint but is opposed to the Pre-Tribulation view. Pretribulationism embraces the idea that the rapture of the church is imminent; it can come at any moment. While certain events may take place before the rapture of the church, there is nothing predicted in Scripture which must happen before the Lord comes for His bride.

7. MID-TRIBULATIONISM LEADS TO DATE SETTING

The Mid-Tribulation view of the rapture actually allows for date-setting. Indeed, if the rapture comes exactly three and one half years after the beginning of the seventieth week of Daniel then there would be no anticipation of it coming at "any time." The passages in Scripture about watching and waiting would be meaningless because there would be no need to either watch or wait. Everyone would know precisely when it would occur. Yet the Bible tells us that we do not know when this event will take place. In fact, Jesus said.

> But about that day or hour no one knows, not even the angels in heaven, nor the Son, but only the Father (Matthew 24:36)

Because nobody can know the Lord told us to "watch." We read.

> Therefore keep watch, because you do not know the day or the hour (Matthew 25:13).

It is clear from Scripture that the date of the rapture cannot be known. However, according to the Mid-Trib scenario the date can be known.

THE EVIDENCE FOR MID-TRIBULATIONISM IS LACKING

There is one final point that should be mentioned. Mid-Tribulationism has been often been criticized because it does not offer much evidence for its position. It is alleged that those who hold the Mid-Tribulation position merely point out problems with the other main views, Pre-Tribulationism and Post-Tribulationism, without presenting much of a positive case for their perspective. It is as though Mid-Tribulationism should be accepted because there are difficulties with these other views. However, the fact that there are problematic issues with the other rapture positions should not cause a person to embrace the Mid-Tribulation view. More evidence needs to be offered for Mid-Tribulationism before it can gain the respect of those holding these other positions.

These are some of the usual objections to the Mid-Tribulation view and they are powerful. We thus conclude that when all the evidence is in, the Mid-Tribulation rapture view does not answer the question as to the timing of the rapture. We must look elsewhere.

SUMMARY TO QUESTION 13
WHAT ARE SOME OF THE BIBLICAL PROBLEMS WITH THE MID-TRIBULATION RAPTURE POSITION?

The mid-tribulation rapture position believes that the church will be taken out of the world before God's wrath hits the earth. This position differs from the pre-tribulation view in that it says the rapture will occur some three and one half years into this final seven-year period. It differs from the post-tribulation view which denies a lengthy interval between the rapture and the Second Coming. Those which hold the pre-tribulation and post-tribulation view have their problems with the mid-tribulation position. Those which hold the pre-tribulation rapture position differ from the mid-tribulation position in the following ways.

To begin with, the seventy weeks of Daniel refer specifically to the future of the nation Israel, not the church! Daniel 9:24 makes this crystal clear. Therefore, the first half of the last seven year period cannot be referring to God's dealing with the church. They are not the subject of the seventy sevens.

In addition, the wrath of God does not start with the seventh trumpet in the Book of Revelation. The pre-tribulation view is that the wrath begins at the opening of the seven seals as recorded in Revelation chapter six. Before this time of wrath even begins, the translation of believers, the rapture of the church, takes place.

There is also the question of the any moment, or imminent, coming of Christ which is denied by the mid-tribulation view. From the pre-tribulation perspective it is the teaching of the New Testament that the rapture could occur at any time. They do not think that a three and one half year period of time has to come to pass before the Lord can come for His bride. It can happen at any moment.

It is alleged that mid-tribulationism mostly points out problems with these other views but offers little positive evidence for its own position. The fact that there are difficulties with the other rapture positions should not cause one to embrace mid-tribulationism as a compromise. This view needs to present more evidence for its case.

QUESTION 14

What Is The Pre-Wrath Rapture View?

A relatively recent view with respect to the timing of the catching up of the church into heaven is known as the "Pre-Wrath" rapture. The main idea behind this theory is that the church will be taken out of the world before the wrath of God strikes the earth. Hence we have the name Pre-Wrath. This complex view of coming events differs from other rapture views in the following ways.

THE RAPTURE TAKES PLACE FIVE AND ONE HALF YEARS INTO THE SEVENTIETH WEEK OF DANIEL

According to the Pre-Wrath position, the rapture of the church occurs late in the seventieth week of Daniel; later than the Pre-Tribulational and Mid-Tribulational view. Believers will be persecuted during the greater part of the last seven-year period in which they will incur the wrath of the beast, the final Antichrist. However, they will be removed from the earth before the wrath of God strikes. God's wrath will last about a year and a half then Jesus Christ will return to the earth.

THE FINAL SEVEN YEARS IS DIVIDED INTO THREE PERIODS

The Pre-Wrath rapture view divides the seventieth week of Daniel, the final seven years before Christ returns, into three periods. Simply stated, they are as follows.

PERIOD ONE:: THE BEGINNING OF SORROWS: THE FIRST THREE AND ONE HALF YEARS

The first period is three and one half years in length and is known as "the beginning of birth pains" or the "beginning of sorrows." The church is on the earth during this period. Jesus spoke about this time period in His Olivet Discourse. He said.

> Jesus answered: "Watch out that no one deceives you. For many will come in my name, claiming, 'I am the Messiah,' and will deceive many. You will hear of wars and rumors of wars, but see to it that you are not alarmed. Such things must happen, but the end is still to come. Nation will rise against nation, and kingdom against kingdom. There will be famines and earthquakes in various places. All these are the beginning of birth pains" (Matthew 24:4-8).

Also during this period the first four seals of the Book of Revelation are opened (Revelation 6:1-8). The "beginning of sorrows" covers the first half of the seventieth week of Daniel.

PERIOD TWO: THE GREAT TRIBULATION

In the middle of the seventieth week of Daniel the next period begins. This is the "great tribulation." Jesus spoke of this coming period.

> For then there will be great distress, unequaled from the beginning of the world until now--and never to be equaled again (Matthew 24:21).

This period is also covered with the breaking of the fifth seal of the Book of Revelation. John wrote.

> When he opened the fifth seal, I saw under the altar the souls of those who had been slain because of the word of God and the testimony they had maintained. They called out in a loud voice, "How long, Sovereign Lord, holy and true, until you

judge the inhabitants of the earth and avenge our blood?"
Then each of them was given a white robe, and they were
told to wait a little longer, until the full number of their
fellow servants, their brothers and sisters, were killed just as
they had been (Revelation 6:9-11)

The great tribulation begins in the middle of Daniel's seventieth
week and ends about half-way through this last three and one half
year period. In other words, the great tribulation lasts for twenty-one
months, or one and three-fourths years.

During this time the church still remains upon the earth. It is important to understand that those who hold the Pre-Wrath view do not
view the entire seventieth week of Daniel as a time of God's wrath.
They believe it is wrong to designate this entire period as such.

When the sixth seal of Revelation is broken it is a warning to the inhabitants of the earth that the third division of Daniel's seventieth week is
about to begin. This is also known as the "Day of the Lord."

The rapture of the church will take place after the breaking of this sixth
seal but before the seventh seal is broken. Right before this last period
begins, the sounding of the seventh trumpet occurs. At that moment
the church is removed from the earth by means of the rapture.

Therefore, the believers in Christ are removed before the wrath of God,
associated with the Day of the Lord, takes place. As stated, this is about
halfway through the last three and one half years before the Second
Coming of Christ. The blessed hope of the church, therefore, is the
removal of believers before the wrath of God is poured out on the
unbelieving world.

PERIOD THREE:: THE DAY OF THE LORD

The third period of the seventieth week of Daniel, the final twenty-one
months, is the Day of the Lord. This is the time when God's wrath is

poured out upon the unbelieving world. This time period would constitute about one fourth of the seventieth week of Daniel.

Thus, the Pre-Wrath view makes the distinction between the beginning of sorrows, the great tribulation and the wrath of God. Consequently, the church can go through the great tribulation without experiencing the wrath of God. The wrath only comes during the last half of the final three and one half years; the Day of the Lord.

To sum up, this view sees the rapture of the church as Post-Tribulational, it comes *after* the great tribulation, but Pre-Wrath, Jesus Christ returns for the believers before the wrath of God strikes the earth.

PERSECUTION OF CHRISTIANS DURING THE GREAT TRIBULATION IS THE WRATH OF SATAN NOT THE WRATH OF GOD

One of the key elements of the Pre-Wrath position is the distinction between the wrath of Satan and the wrath of God. God's wrath is not poured out on the world until the seventh of the seven seals is broken. The persecution by the final Antichrist will be the wrath of Satan; not the wrath of God. We read of this in the Book of Revelation.

> Therefore rejoice, you heavens and you who dwell in them! But woe to the earth and the sea, because the devil has gone down to you! He is filled with fury, because he knows that his time is short (Revelation 12:12).

The wrath of Satan against the Christians ends when the sign of the sun, moon, and stars appears in the heavens. Jesus said.

> Immediately after the distress of those days the sun will be darkened, and the moon will not give its light; the stars will fall from the sky, and the heavenly bodies will be shaken (Matthew 24:29).

At that time, the distress or tribulation of those days, the believers in Christ will be raptured. Once this event takes place, then the wrath of

God will begin against those who are left behind. This wrath will end with the battle of Armageddon.

To sum up, the rapture will take place twenty-one months into the second half of the seventieth week of Daniel. After the rapture of the church occurs there will be twenty-one months of the wrath of God being poured out upon the inhabitants of the earth.

THERE IS NO IMMINENT COMING OF JESUS CHRIST FOR BELIEVERS

Like all of the views of the rapture, except the Pre-Tribulation position, the doctrine of the imminent, or an "any moment," rapture is denied by those holding the Pre-Wrath theory. Indeed, according to this position, there are a number of events which must come to pass before the church can be caught up into heaven.

In particular, there will be the persecution of God's people by the final Antichrist. This persecution will last a number of years. Thus, it is wrong for Christians to be looking for the rapture at any moment because there are certain things which must be fulfilled before the rapture of the church can take place.

It is also stressed that the rapture could not have been imminent throughout church history because the seventieth week of Daniel begins when the final Antichrist makes a covenant with the nation of Israel.

Since Israel did not exist as a constituted state with recognized borders until 1948, the rapture could not have taken place until Israel was back in the land and reacquired statehood. Therefore, the rapture could not have been imminent during the long history of the church.

THE RAPTURE OCCURS THE SAME DAY THAT WRATH STRIKES

Those who hold to the Pre-Wrath view understand the rapture of the church occurring on the same day as the wrath of God begins to strike the earth. Noah's flood is used as an illustration of what will happen. The Bible says that Noah entered the ark the same day in which the flood began the judgment of God. We read in Genesis.

> In the six hundredth year of Noah's life, on the seventeenth day of the second month--on that day all the springs of the great deep burst forth, and the floodgates of the heavens were opened. And rain fell on the earth forty days and forty nights. On that very day Noah and his sons, Shem, Ham and Japheth, together with his wife and the wives of his three sons, entered the ark (Genesis 7:11-13).

In the same manner, the wrath of God cannot occur until the day the believers are removed from the earth. With the sounding of the seventh trumpet in the Book of Revelation the rapture takes place and then the wrath of God immediately begins.

THIS VIEW IS HELD BY GODLY PEOPLE

Like the other views with respect to the timing of the rapture, the Pre-Wrath view is held by serious Bible-believing Christians. Consequently it should be examined to see if it can best explain the timing of the catching up of the church. While it is the newest of the theories its newness should not eliminate it from being considered.

SUMMARY TO QUESTION 14
WHAT IS THE PRE-WRATH RAPTURE VIEW?

The pre-wrath rapture theory is a relatively recent understanding of the timing of the rapture of the church. This complex theory believes the translation, or catching up, of the church, occurs about three fourths of the way through the last seven year period, or the seventieth week of Daniel. This is before the wrath of God strikes the earth. The previous five and one half years of this seven year period are not seen as the wrath of God but rather the wrath of man. It is only when the wrath of God is about to hit the earth that the church is removed. The removal of the church is at the time of the sounding of the seventh trumpet in the Book of Revelation. The church is removed and the wrath then begins.

The pre-wrath view divides the last seven years into three periods. The first is the "Beginning of Sorrows" which lasts three and one half years. The second period is the Great Tribulation which lasts twenty-one months or one and three-fourths years. The final period, the Day of the Lord, also lasts twenty-one months. It is during this time that the wrath of God is poured out on the world.

Since the pre-wrath view says the wrath of God does not begin until late into the seventieth week of Daniel, it holds that the rapture need not occur before that time. The terrible problems that happen on the earth earlier in the last seven year period can be attributed to the wrath of the Satan working through his man, the Antichrist. This is an important distinction. While the people of the earth suffer tremendously during those first five and one half years this suffering should not be ascribed to God. His wrath does not begin until the end of the seven year period.

Accordingly, like every view except the pre-tribulation position, the pre-wrath view holds that the New Testament does not teach that Christ can come at any moment for the church. In other words, there is no imminent coming of Christ taught. The believers will have to experience severe persecution before Christ comes back for the church. When He does return it will be to rescue them from the coming wrath. As is true with these other views of the timing of the rapture of the church, there are godly people which embrace this perspective. This being the case, we need to see how this view matches up with the Scripture.

QUESTION 15

What Are Some Of The Biblical Problems With The Pre-Wrath Rapture View?

The Pre-Wrath rapture view is the newest of the theories with respect to the timing of the rapture of the church. As can be imagined, there have been objections to this new point of view.

We can look at the areas of agreement between the various theories as well as the specific objections which each of the other positions would make to the Pre-Wrath claims.

A COMPARISON BETWEEN PRE-WRATH AND THE MID-TRIBULATION RAPTURE VIEW

Those who hold the Mid-Tribulation position would agree with the Pre-Wrath view that there is an interval of time between the rapture of the church and the end of the seventieth week of Daniel.

However, the Mid-Tribulation position would differ with the Pre-Wrath view on the *timing* of the rapture. Pre-Wrath puts this great event about twenty one months later into the seventieth week of Daniel.

A COMPARISON BETWEEN PRE-WRATH AND THE POST-TRIBULATION VIEW

The Post-Tribulational point of view would also accept many of the Pre-Wrath arguments. Indeed, some of critics of the Pre-Wrath rapture position see this theory as another twist on the Post-Tribulation theory since there is not much difference between them.

Pre-Wrath and Post-Tribulationism would deny that the coming of Jesus Christ could be at "any moment." However, the Post-Tribulation supporters would disagree with the Pre-Wrath position that an interval of time is needed between the rapture and the end of the seventieth week of Daniel. The Post-Tribulational position has the rapture at the very end of the seven year period rather than twenty-one months before the end.

Consequently, there are some differences between these two views.

AGREEMENTS BETWEEN PRE-TRIBULATIONISM AND PRE-WRATH

There are certain areas in which the Pre-Tribulation theory agrees with those who hold to the Pre-Wrath rapture. For one thing, each of these rapture theories believes the rapture will occur *before* the wrath of God is poured out upon the earth.

Furthermore, each theory also believes that the "Day of the Lord" is a time when God's wrath comes upon the unbelieving people of the earth; the non-Christians. The differences occur when we attempt to determine exactly when the wrath of God is poured out.

MOST RAPTURE POSITIONS BELIEVE THAT THE RAPTURE IS PRE-WRATH

There is a point that should be made regarding the various views of the rapture of the church and the wrath of God. Almost everyone who deals with the rapture question believes that the rapture of the church will come *before* the wrath of God. Indeed, this is the view of Pre-Tribulationism, Mid-Tribulationism, and even some of those who hold the Post-Tribulation position.

Therefore, almost any view of the rapture of the church could rightly be called "Pre-Wrath" since it is agreed that believers in Jesus Christ are delivered from the coming wrath of God. In this sense, the Pre-Wrath view is certainly not unique.

Thus, the idea that the rapture occurs "Pre-Wrath" is not some new discovery. What is unique about the Pre-Wrath view is the *timing* of the rapture.

In sum, the Pre-Wrath position has some arguments which each of the other views would embrace as well as having arguments which each of the other views would not accept.

OBJECTIONS TO THE PRE-WRATH VIEW FROM PRE-TRIBULATIONISM

Those who hold to a Pre-Tribulation rapture position, such as the author, have a number of points where we disagree with the Pre-Wrath view. The main objections can be summed up as follows.

OBJECTION 1: PRE-TRIBULATIONISM SAYS THE BEGINNING OF THE WRATH OF GOD OCCURS WITH THE BREAKING OF THE FIRST SEAL

Both the Pre-Tribulation rapture theory and the Pre-Wrath position believe that this final seven-year period, the seventieth week of Daniel, begins with the breaking of the first seal as is recorded in Revelation chapter six. They also agree that the breaking of this first seal brings calamity to the earth.

The difference between these views concerns the one responsible for this terrible calamity. The Pre-Wrath view believes it is Satan, through the final Antichrist, which is responsible for the beginning of these great judgments. According to the Pre-Wrath view, the wrath of God does not begin to strike the earth until the seventh of the seven seals is broken. This does not occur until about five and one half years into the final seven year period.

On the other hand, the Pre-Tribulation view believes it is God who institutes His wrath at the time of the breaking of the *first* seal. All of these recorded events which follow are a direct result of God's wrath being poured out upon the earth.

In fact, Scripture makes it clear that God's judgment is carried out with the breaking of the very first seal. Indeed, it is Jesus Christ Himself that breaks these seals. The riders on the four horses accomplish *His* judgment upon the earth.

Furthermore, this judgment is initiated by the four living creatures which descend from *God's* presence. These four living creatures are described as follows.

> Surrounding the throne were twenty-four other thrones, and seated on them were twenty-four elders. They were dressed in white and had crowns of gold on their heads. From the throne came flashes of lightning, rumblings and peals of thunder. In front of the throne, seven lamps were blazing. These are the seven spirits of God. Also in front of the throne there was what looked like a sea of glass, clear as crystal. In the center, around the throne, were four living creatures, and they were covered with eyes, in front and in back (Revelation 4:4-6)

These four living creatures command each of the four horsemen to "come." Scripture says.

> I watched as the Lamb opened the first of the seven seals. Then I heard one of the four living creatures say in a voice like thunder, "Come!" I looked, and there before me was a white horse! Its rider held a bow, and he was given a crown, and he rode out as a conqueror bent on conquest (Revelation 6:1-2)

Thus, the judgments of the four horsemen of the apocalypse are *initiated* by the Lamb, Jesus Christ, through the four living creatures which are in *His* presence. The fact that the Lord is using human agents to accomplish His purposes does not mean this is the wrath of humans which is taking place.

THERE ARE EXAMPLES OF GOD USING HUMANS TO CARRY OUT HIS WORK OF JUDGMENT

The entire seventieth week of Daniel is a time when God's judgment is poured out upon the earth. In some of the judgments God uses humans to accomplish His purposes. This is not something unique to this time period. In fact, there are many examples of this type of judgment in Scripture.

Indeed, on the Day of Pentecost, Simon Peter told the crowd which had gathered about who was responsible for the death of Jesus Christ. We read him saying the following.

This man was handed over to you by God's deliberate plan and foreknowledge; and you, with the help of wicked men, put him to death by nailing him to the cross (Acts 2:23)

While Jesus Christ did indeed die at the hands of evil people, ultimately His death was in the pre-determined plan of God. Thus, God worked out this plan through unbelievers.

The Apostle Paul spoke of a thorn in the flesh which distracted him from the ministry. He called it a "messenger of Satan." He wrote.

For because of these surpassingly great revelations. Therefore, in order to keep me from becoming conceited, I was given a thorn in my flesh, a messenger of Satan, to torment me. Three times I pleaded with the Lord to take it away from me (2 Corinthians 12:7).

While the thorn in the flesh was a messenger of Satan, Paul said that ultimately it was given to him by God to serve a higher purpose. Therefore, God can indeed work His purposes through evil agents.

Thus, the seal judgments of the first part of the seventieth week of Daniel should be seen as the wrath of God taking place. While the judgments become more intense as the seven year period progresses, they are all, nevertheless, judgments of God which are instituted by the

Lord and by Him alone. Consequently, this period begins with great tribulation and then goes on to greater tribulation.

THE DAY OF THE LORD HAS ARRIVED BY THE SIXTH SEAL

There is something else. Contrary to the Pre-Wrath view, the sixth seal cannot be anticipating the coming "Day of the Lord;" that great time of wrath which is *about* to happen. Scripture says.

> They called to the mountains and the rocks, "Fall on us and hide us from the face of him who sits on the throne and from the wrath of the Lamb! For the great day of their wrath has come, and who can withstand it?" (Revelation 6:16-17)

This is not anticipating God's wrath; it is experiencing it! Otherwise, it would have the people on earth announcing the soon-coming of something that the Bible says will take them entirely by surprise! Paul wrote about that time period.

> For you know very well that the day of the Lord will come like a thief in the night (1 Thessalonians 5:2)

This day will come as a complete surprise since a thief, by definition, is not anticipated. Consequently the unbelievers would not be able to predict when this time of judgment would begin.

Peter wrote the same thing about the day of the Lord. He said.

> But the day of the Lord will come like a thief. The heavens will disappear with a roar; the elements will be destroyed by fire, and the earth and everything done in it will be laid bare (2 Peter 3:10).

Thus, the sixth seal has the earth-dwellers recognizing what has *already* taken place. Hence, the "Day of the Lord" has already arrived by the time the sixth seal is opened. However, the worst is still yet to come.

OBJECTION 2: THE BIBLE DOES NOT MAKE A COMPLETE DISTINCTION BETWEEN THE GREAT TRIBULATION AND THE DAY OF THE LORD

For the Pre-Wrath rapture view to be correct there must be no overlapping between the great tribulation and the Day of the Lord. Yet the Bible does not allow for this. In fact, Jesus spoke of the great tribulation as a time of unparalleled trouble which will strike the earth.

> For then there will be great distress, unequaled from the beginning of the world until now--and never to be equaled again (Matthew 24:21)

In writing about the future "Day of the Lord" the prophet Joel called it a time of unparalleled trouble.

> Blow the trumpet in Zion; sound the alarm on my holy hill. Let all who live in the land tremble, for the day of the LORD is coming. It is close at hand--a day of darkness and gloom, a day of clouds and blackness. Like dawn spreading across the mountains a large and mighty army comes, such as never was in ancient times nor ever will be in ages to come (Joel 2:1-2).

Daniel wrote about this future time of unparalleled distress. He explained it this manner.

> At that time Michael, the great prince who protects your people, will arise. There will be a time of distress such as has not happened from the beginning of nations until then. But at that time your people--everyone whose name is found written in the book--will be delivered (Daniel 12:1).

The great tribulation is a time of unparalleled trouble as is the future "Day of the Lord." There cannot be two future times of unparalleled trouble which will come upon the earth. Therefore, we cannot completely separate the great tribulation from the Day of the Lord as is done with the Pre-Wrath view.

This brings up another problem. If the great tribulation is merely a time of *human wrath* then how can it be called an unparalleled time of trouble? Certainly God's wrath is far more severe than any human wrath. Hence the distinction between the great tribulation and the Day of the Lord cannot be maintained.

OBJECTION 3: PRE-WRATH DENIES THE BIBLICAL DOCTRINE OF IMMINENCY

Those who believe the rapture occurs before the seventieth week of Daniel, the Pre-Tribulation view, argue that the early church had the belief that Jesus Christ could come at any moment. Indeed, Paul wrote of himself as a possible participant in the rapture. He said.

> For the Lord himself will come down from heaven, with a loud command, with the voice of the archangel and with the trumpet call of God, and the dead in Christ will rise first. After that, we who are still alive and are left will be caught up together with them in the clouds to meet the Lord in the air. And so we will be with the Lord forever (1 Thessalonians 4:16-17).

This passage shows that the imminent coming of Christ was expected by the first generation of Christians. If this is the case, then the Pre-Wrath view is not correct.

Earlier in that same letter Paul pictured the church waiting for Jesus to rescue the believers from the time of wrath.

> And to wait for his Son from heaven, whom he raised from the dead—Jesus, who rescues us from the coming wrath (1 Thessalonians 1:10)

Again, there seems to be an expectation that Christ may come at any moment. Jesus will rescue believers "away from" the coming wrath. Paul included himself in this group who would be rescued.

Of course, one could argue that the Lord would rescue people by means of protecting them when the wrath took place. However, other passages in this same letter point to the deliverance of the Lord as Him taking His church out of the world rather than protecting them in it (for example see 1 Thessalonians 4:13-18).

If Paul had taught these believers that the great tribulation, or even some part of it, must take place first, then it is difficult to see how these Christians could be described as expectantly awaiting Christ's return. Indeed, they would have been described as preparing themselves for the great tribulation and the horrific events connected with it. That would be their immediate expectation.

However, the Pre-Wrath rapture view would have the believers waiting almost *five and one half years* before the Lord comes back for the Christians. Yet, we read in the Book of James how the coming of the Lord is "at hand." He wrote.

> Be patient, then, brothers and sisters, until the Lord's coming. See how the farmer waits for the land to yield its valuable crop, patiently waiting for the autumn and spring rains. You too, be patient and stand firm, because the Lord's coming is near. Don't grumble against one another, brothers and sisters, or you will be judged. The Judge is standing at the door! (James 5:7-9).

These passages seem to indicate the possibility of an *immediate* return of the Lord rather than some sort of delay which would last for years.

While things such as Israel's existence as a national entity may seem like a difficulty for the view of imminency of the coming of Christ, it is not. The doctrine of imminency says that the rapture is the next scheduled event on the prophetic calendar. Though other events *may* intervene there are no other events which *must* intervene

OBJECTION 4: THE BLESSED HOPE IS MISPLACED IN PRE-WRATH

According to the Pre-Wrath view the "blessed hope" is the deliverance by God from the time of wrath which is coming upon the world. However, the Scripture says that the blessed hope for the believer is looking for the coming of Jesus Christ. It is for the purpose of being with Him in His wonderful presence. It is not merely the hope of escaping temporary suffering here upon the earth; no matter how difficult the suffering may be. Pre-Wrath misplaces that hope.

CONCLUSION: THE PRE-WRATH VIEW HAS TOO MANY PROBLEMS

While many sincere people hold the Pre-wrath view we do not believe that it is the best way to understand the timing of the rapture. Indeed, this complex theory does not adequately explain *all* of the biblical evidence.

SUMMARY TO QUESTION 15
WHAT ARE SOME OF THE BIBLICAL PROBLEMS TO THE PRE-WRATH RAPTURE VIEW?

The pre-wrath rapture view is the newest of theories with respect to the timing of the catching up of the church. It sees the rapture occurring about five and one half years into the final seven year period or the seventieth week of Daniel. This view sees the final seven year period divided into three parts. The first part, "the Beginning of Sorrows" lasts three and one half years. Next is the Great Tribulation period which lasts twenty-one months. Then, the final period takes place which also lasts twenty-one months; the Day of the Lord. It is during the Day of the Lord that the wrath of God is poured out upon the world. Immediately before the Day of the Lord the seventh trumpet of the Book of Revelation sounds which signals the rapture of the church. The church, therefore, escapes the wrath of God by means of the rapture.

There have been a number of objections against this new theory. Those who hold the pre-tribulation rapture position have the following areas of disagreement with the pre-wrath position. According to the pre-tribulation view, the coming of Christ is imminent. The early church was looking for an, "any moment," rapture; they weren't expecting five and one half years of trouble before the rapture took place. Thus, there is a basic disagreement as to whether or not believers should be looking for the coming of the Lord now or looking for the antichrist and the various horrific events contained in the Book of Revelation. This includes intense persecution of believers.

Furthermore, the pre-tribulation view believes that the wrath of God begins with the opening of the first of the seven seals as recorded in Revelation chapter six. The pre-wrath view sees the first six seals as the wrath of Satan which is directed through the Antichrist. God's wrath does not begin until later. This is a major area of disagreement.

The pre-tribulation view sees the entire seven year period as one where God's wrath strikes the earth. While the first part of the tribulation may be less intense than the second half, it is still the wrath of God which is striking the earth during the entire period. Indeed, it is Jesus Christ who breaks each of the seven seals on the scroll and His agents, the four living creatures, initiate this judgment. Thus, it is wrong to call this judgment "the wrath of man" rather than the wrath of God. The mid-tribulation position would agree with many of the arguments of the pre-wrath advocates. They, however, would see the wrath beginning a few years earlier. This is why they see the rapture occurring three and one half years into the period rather than five and one half years.

This briefly sums up the basic biblical objections to the pre-wrath rapture position.

QUESTION 16

What Is The Post-Tribulation Rapture View?

One of the most popular views with respect to the timing of the rapture of the church is known as Post-Tribulationism. Simply stated, this position holds that the church will be caught up to meet the Lord in the air as He returns to the earth *after* the great tribulation period.

This being the case, the church, which consists of both Jews and Gentiles, must undergo the time of trouble which the rest of the people on earth experience. During this period the church will suffer great persecution but will be more or less exempt from the wrath of God which strikes the inhabitants of the earth.

According to the Post-Tribulation view, the rapture of the church and the Second Coming of Christ are seen as two parts of a single complex event. The rapture occurs as the Lord is descending from heaven. Jesus meets the living saints in the air and together they come to the earth.

Thus, the Post-Tribulation view is different from the Pre-Tribulation, Mid-Tribulation, and Pre-Wrath view with respect to the *timing* of the rapture in that there is no interval between the catching up of the church and the Second Coming. In fact, they are seen as one event.

Those who hold to the Post-Tribulation rapture position do not all share the same view as to what occurs *after* the Second Coming of Christ. Some believe there will be a literal thousand year reign of Jesus

Christ upon the earth. They are known as pre-millennialists because they believe the return of Christ will occur *before* a literal Millennium.

There are other Post-Tribulationists who do not believe that when Christ returns there will be a literal thousand year time of peace on the earth. They are known as amillenialists; those who do not believe in a literal Millennium on the earth. Amillenialists believe the eternal state follows the return of Christ. Yet all Post-Tribulationists see the coming of Christ and the rapture as a single complex event.

THE CASE FOR POST-TRIBULATIONISM

We will state the main arguments which are usually given in support of Post-Tribulationism. As always, we will try to find the best evidence used by those who embrace this system.

THE ARGUMENT FROM HISTORY

The historical argument is often the first one listed by those who advocate Post-Tribulationism. Simply stated, it is claimed that the view of Post-Tribulationism has been the historic view of the church. The great majority of Bible commentators, no matter what denomination they belong to or theological system they hold, have believed and taught that the church will *not* escape the great tribulation period. This is still true today. There must be some reason for this. If Post-Tribulationism is not true then some explanation must be given as to why the great majority of Bible students have held to it.

THERE IS ONLY ONE COMING OF CHRIST AND IT IS POST-TRIBULATIONAL

Post-Tribulationism stresses that there is only *one* coming of Christ, not two. If this can be demonstrated, then the matter is solved. The rapture of the church occurs with the Second Coming of Jesus Christ and this coming is *after* the great tribulation.

If there is more than one coming of Christ, then there must be some explicit evidence for it. However, it is claimed that there is not one passage of Scripture that clearly teaches two separate comings of Jesus Christ. This being the case, whenever the Bible speaks of the coming of Christ it is always speaking of the same event. The burden of proof is on those who believe in more than one coming.

Furthermore, the Bible clearly states that the coming of Jesus Christ to the earth is *after* the tribulation.

Jesus said.

> Immediately after the distress of those days the sun will be darkened, and the moon will not give its light; the stars will fall from the sky, and the heavenly bodies will be shaken. Then will appear the sign of the Son of Man in heaven. And then all the peoples of the earth will mourn when they see the Son of Man coming on the clouds of heaven, with power and great glory (Matthew 24:29-30).

To sum up, the Scriptures teach one coming of Christ and that coming is after the tribulation or the distress of those final days.

3. THE RESURRECTION AND THE RETURN OF CHRIST HAPPEN AT THE SAME TIME

Another argument for the Post-Tribulation rapture has to do with passages which equate the resurrection of believers with the coming of Christ. Indeed, the Bible often speaks of the resurrection and the return of the Lord in the same passage. In the Old Testament we read the following.

> But your dead will live, LORD; their bodies will rise-- let those who dwell in the dust wake up and shout for joy-- your dew is like the dew of the morning; the earth will give birth to her dead. Go, my people, enter your rooms and shut the doors behind you; hide yourselves for a little while until his wrath has passed by. See, the LORD is coming out of his

dwelling to punish the people of the earth for their sins. The earth will disclose the blood shed on it; the earth will conceal its slain no longer (Isaiah 26:19-21).

Here the coming of the Lord is linked to the resurrection of the righteous. We find Jesus doing the same thing. In the gospel of Matthew, He is recorded as saying the following about His return to the earth.

And he will send his angels with a loud trumpet call, and they will gather his elect from the four winds, from one end of the heavens to the other (Matthew 24:30-31).

At Jesus' coming the elect are gathered. This includes the dead.

In writing about the resurrection, Paul also placed it at the same time as the coming of Christ. He wrote to the Corinthians.

But each in turn: Christ, the firstfruits; then, when he comes, those who belong to him (1 Corinthians 15:23).

When Paul wrote to the Philippians he said something similar. He stated that the transformation of our bodies will be at the coming of Jesus Christ.

But our citizenship is in heaven. And we eagerly await a Savior from there, the Lord Jesus Christ, who, by the power that enables him to bring everything under his control, will transform our lowly bodies so that they will be like his glorious body (Philippians 3:20,21).

These passages seem to make it plain that the coming of the Lord occurs at the same time as the resurrection of the dead. To many, this is clear evidence of a Post-Tribulation rapture. The reasoning is simple. Everyone agrees that the Second Coming of Christ occurs after the great tribulation; it is post-tribulational.

It is also agreed that the rapture event involves the resurrection of the dead. Since Scripture says the dead are raised at the coming of Christ and this coming is after the great tribulation period then the rapture must occur after the great tribulation.

It is further argued that while these passages are proof-texts for the Post-Tribulation position there are no proof-texts whatsoever that separate the coming of Christ into two stages; one coming of Christ for His church and another coming is with His church. The time of the rapture of the church is never distinguished from the time of Jesus' Second Coming. Therefore, the obvious conclusion is that the rapture occurs at the time of the Second Coming.

4. THE RESURRECTION OF THE RIGHTEOUS IS A SINGLE EVENT

There are three passages which seem to prove that the resurrection of the all of the righteous believers occurs at the same time. First, Daniel the prophet when writing about the resurrection of the dead put it this way.

> At that time Michael, the great prince who protects your people, will arise. There will be a time of distress such as has not happened from the beginning of nations until then. But at that time your people--everyone whose name is found written in the book--will be delivered. Multitudes who sleep in the dust of the earth will awake: some to everlasting life, others to shame and everlasting contempt (Daniel 12:1-2).

This indicates the righteous dead will *all* be raised at the same time.

JESUS SAID THE BELIEVERS WOULD BE RAISED TOGETHER

Next we discover that Jesus Himself spoke of the "hour" of the resurrection when the believers would be raised together. He said.

> Do not be amazed at this, for a time is coming when all who are in their graves will hear his voice and come out--those

> who have done what is good will rise to live, and those
> who have done what is evil will rise to be condemned
> (John 5:28-29)

There is every indication that all believers are raised at this coming "hour." The righteous are raised first then the unbelievers are raised. We learn of this in the Book of Revelation. It says that the unbelieving dead were not raised until one thousand years *after* the righteous were raised. John wrote.

> The rest of the dead did not come to life until the thousand
> years were ended. This is the first resurrection (Revelation
> 20:5).

Again, this indicates the righteous dead are all raised at the same time. This is long before the unbelievers are raised.

These passages appear to conclusively state that the resurrection of believers occurs at the same moment. This is significant for the question of the timing of the rapture. Since Paul clearly said that the dead are raised immediately *before* the church is caught up to meet the Lord in the air, then it seems obvious that the rapture must take place when the Lord returns to the earth.

If the rapture occurs any time before the Lord returns, as in the Pre-Tribulation, Mid-Tribulation, or Pre-Wrath view, then what will happen to the people who become believers after the church is caught up to meet the Lord? There does not seem to be any time where they can be raised from the dead if they are martyred.

5. RAPTURE PASSAGES ARE LINKED WITH PASSAGES ON THE SECOND COMING

There are a number of passages where the rapture is directly linked to the Second Coming of Jesus Christ. In the first chapter of Second Thessalonians we read the following words.

All this is evidence that God's judgment is right, and as a result you will be counted worthy of the kingdom of God, for which you are suffering. God is just: He will pay back trouble to those who trouble you and give relief to you who are troubled, and to us as well. This will happen when the Lord Jesus is revealed from heaven in blazing fire with his powerful angels. He will punish those who do not know God and do not obey the gospel of our Lord Jesus. They will be punished with everlasting destruction and shut out from the presence of the Lord and from the glory of his might on the day he comes to be glorified in his holy people and to be marveled at among all those who have believed. This includes you, because you believed our testimony to you (2 Thessalonians 1:5-10).

This passage equates the coming of the Lord for the believers, the rapture, with the vengeance He will pour out upon the unbelievers, the Second Coming of Christ. In other words, *one event* is in view.

6. THE SAME GREEK WORDS ARE USED TO DESCRIBE THE RAPTURE AND THE SECOND COMING

We also find that the same Greek words, *parousia, epiphaneia* and *apokalupsis*, which describe the rapture of the church, are also used in other contexts to describe the Second Coming of Christ. Since each of these three words describe both the rapture and the Second Coming the logical conclusion seems to be they are describing the same event. The burden of proof is on those who want to understand it otherwise.

7. THERE IS NO IMMINENT RETURN OF CHRIST

Another formidable argument in favor of Post-Tribulationism is the seeming impossibility of the imminent return of Jesus Christ during the early years of the church. From the New Testament, we find that a number of events would have to take place before Christ could return.

They include, but are not limited to, the following.

Jesus said that Peter must grow old and die. Consequently, the rapture of the church could not happen until the death of Peter. This would involve a period of time.

Jesus also said that the gospel must be preached to the entire world. Until the entire world was evangelized, it would not be possible for rapture of the church to occur. Again, this seems to rule out the idea of an, "any moment" rapture.

The Apostle Paul said the Holy Spirit showed him that he must visit Rome. Thus, until Paul set his foot in Rome the rapture of the church could not take place.

This is just a sample of what the writers of Scripture predicted must occur in the future. Since these things had to take place, it was not possible for an imminent or any moment return of the Lord for the church. Therefore, it is folly to say that the rapture was looked upon as an "any moment" event for the early church. It was not.

THE NATURE OF THE TRIBULATION ITSELF GIVES EVIDENCE FOR A POST-TRIB RAPTURE

There are those who teach that this present age in which we live is "the tribulation." Thus, the church is already passing through tribulation. Consequently, the "great tribulation" consists of the trials and persecutions which the church is experiencing during this present age. There was great persecution or tribulation for the early church and it has continued until today.

Others say this tribulation is not unique to this age. Indeed, they say it actually goes all the way back to Adam. Whether one accepts that the great tribulation goes all the way back to Adam or that it is unique to the church age, the end result is that the church will pass through the time of tribulation before Christ returns. While it may be more intense before the Lord returns, tribulation is occurring right now. If this is the correct definition of the great tribulation then any rapture of the saints will occur after the tribulation period or at the very least, during it. However, there are other posttribulationists which see the great tribulation as a future time of trouble which will occur shortly before the return of Christ. They do not believe that this particular period has occurred as of yet. *Most* posttribulationists would hold to this position.

Thus, there are differing viewpoints among posttribulationists with respect to their definition of what it means for the church to pass through the tribulation. One position understands the tribulation to refer to trouble and persecutions which characterizes the present age in which we live. Some even claim this period goes all the way back to Adam. Others who hold the Post-Tribulation view regard the tribulation as something in the future.

9. BELIEVERS ARE NEVER PROMISED ESCAPE FROM TRIBULATION

There is also the issue of believers escaping persecution and tribulation. The Scripture does not teach that Christians are immune to such things. In fact, Jesus said that Christians would face troubles.

> I have told you these things, so that in me you may have peace. In this world you will have trouble. But take heart! I have overcome the world (John 16:33).

The Apostle Paul made the same point.

> In fact, everyone who wants to live a godly life in Christ Jesus will be persecuted (2 Timothy 3:12).

We find this persecution, tribulation, and even martyrdom described in the Book of Acts.

Even if there was an unprecedented time of trouble, like the great tribulation, there has to be clear indications in Scripture that the church would escape this period. To those who hold the Post-Tribulation view, they do not believe the evidence is there.

10. THERE ARE BELIEVERS ON EARTH DURING THE FUTURE TRIBULATION PERIOD

Those who hold to the Post-Tribulation view emphasize that God's people can remain on earth while escaping His wrath. Scripture gives examples of God's *protection* of His own in the midst of judgments. Indeed, the children of Israel were protected from the various plagues which struck Egypt; they were not removed from the scene. Something similar will take place during the great tribulation.

Consequently, even if there is a time of unprecedented trouble in the future, the Lord can shelter His people during this period. Thus, there is no need to remove them by means of the rapture.

Furthermore, *every* rapture theory acknowledges that there are believers, both Jews and Gentiles, on earth during this time before Jesus returns. For example, we read.

> Then the dragon was enraged at the woman and went off to wage war against the rest of her offspring--those who keep God's commands and hold fast their testimony about Jesus (Revelation 12:17).

Therefore, the Bible itself testifies that there are Christians on the earth when the great tribulation occurs. This fact, according to many Post-Tribulationists, settles the issue.

11. THE WRATH OF GOD DOES NOT OCCUR UNTIL LATE IN THE SEVENTIETH WEEK OF DANIEL

One of the central arguments of the Post-Tribulation rapture position concerns the wrath of God. Those who hold the Post-Tribulation view usually place the wrath of God at the very end of the tribulation. They do not see the wrath of God as being poured out at the beginning of the period as Pre-Tribulationists do.

SCRIPTURE MAKES NO CLEAR DISTINCTION BETWEEN ISRAEL AND THE CHURCH

Most of the people who hold to the Post-Tribulation view do not keep the nation of Israel and the New Testament church as distinct entities. Rather they see the church as a continuation of Israel or the "new Israel" because Israel forfeited their promises of God by rejecting Jesus the Messiah. These promises now belong to the New Testament church.

In support of this idea, it is argued that during the great tribulation period we find both people from the nation of Israel as well as the church saints on the earth. Each of these groups is experiencing the sufferings of this unprecedented time.

Contrary to other views, they do not see the great tribulation as a time in which God mainly deals with the nation of Israel.

THE LAST TRUMPET OF FIRST CORINTHIANS IS THE SAME AS THE LAST TRUMPET IN REVELATION

There is also the argument about the timing of the trumpet. In First Corinthians we read about rapture occurring at the time of the "last trumpet." Paul wrote.

> Listen, I tell you a mystery: We will not all sleep, but we will all be changed-- in a flash, in the twinkling of an eye, at the last trumpet. For the trumpet will sound, the dead will be raised imperishable, and we will be changed (1 Corinthians 15:51-52).

This last trumpet is defined in Revelation. John put it this way.

> The seventh angel sounded his trumpet, and there were loud voices in heaven, which said: "The kingdom of the world has

become the kingdom of our Lord and of his Messiah, and he
will reign for ever and ever" (Revelation 11:15)

Furthermore, the context in Revelation 11 indicates they are the same
trumpet. Indeed, we find that this seventh trumpet takes place the time
of the resurrection of the dead. We read.

The nations were angry, and your wrath has come. The time
has come for judging the dead, and for rewarding your servants the prophets and your people who revere your name,
both great and small--and for destroying those who destroy
the earth (Revelation 11:18)

Consequently, John is describing the same event which Paul wrote
about in First Thessalonians 4 and First Corinthians 15; a Post-
Tribulation rapture and a resurrection of the dead believers.

This sums up some of the main arguments which are used by those
who believe that the rapture of the church takes place at the end of the
great tribulation period or the seventieth week of Daniel. These arguments have convinced many people that the Post-Tribulation rapture
position is the best way to understand the totality of the evidence. As
we have stressed, there are many good Bible-believers who hold this
position.

SUMMARY TO QUESTION 16
WHAT IS THE POST-TRIBULATION RAPTURE VIEW?

The post-tribulation theory claims to be the oldest of the different
views with respect to the rapture of the church. This view contends
the church will go through the entire period of tribulation and suffering before Jesus Christ returns to the earth. They see the rapture as
part of the Second Coming of Christ. While they are distinct events,
they occur at basically the same time. Consequently, they are two
parts of one complex event. Those who hold the post-tribulation rapture view often say that this has been the historic view of the church.

They contend that there is a reason as to why most Bible-believers throughout history have held that the church must endure this time of suffering. The reason, it is argued, is because this is what the Bible teaches on the subject.

There is also the argument from the coming of the Lord. Scripture says there is only one coming of Christ. Those who argue for more than one coming of Christ must give sufficient evidence as to why we should believe there is more than one time Christ comes; once for the church and then another time to judge the world. Those who hold the post-tribulation view believe the evidence is not there for an interval between the rapture and the Second Coming.

Indeed, they say there are no proof-texts to be found for the idea of two comings of Christ; one for the believers and one with the believers. Consequently the rapture of the church and the coming of Christ should be seen as part of the same end-time event. In addition, Scripture itself speaks of the return of Christ with the resurrection of believers in the same passage. The Bible also says the rapture event involves the resurrection of believers. Since the believers are raised at the same time as the coming of Christ this must mean the catching up of the church occurs when Christ returns to the earth.

Thus, to many people, these passages are the closest things to proof-texts for a post-tribulation rapture. Furthermore, since the same Greek words which are used for the rapture are also used for the Second Coming the logical result would be to see them as the same event. Those who wish to see them as two distinct events have the burden of proof on them.

Christians in the past, as well as in the present, have experienced trials and tribulations. Therefore, there does not seem to be any reason as to why one future generation of Christians would be exempt from such difficulties. This would be the case even if there was a time of unprecedented tribulation the world would experience.

In addition, we do find believers on the earth during the Great Tribulation period. The Book of Revelation says that the saints and the elect are on the earth during this time of trouble. This solves the issue as to whether the church will go through this difficult period.

There is also the fact that the Bible says that the resurrection of the righteous occurs at the same time. Since Paul said that the dead are raised immediately before the church is raptured this would seem to clinch the case for a post-tribulational catching up of the believers. The dead are raised when Christ returns and according to many post-tribulationists, judgment immediately follows.

The wrath of God is also said to be limited to the very end of the seventieth week of Daniel, the Great Tribulation period. The greater part of this period consists of persecution from Satan through his man, the man of sin, the antichrist. While Christians will be on earth during this final period of God's wrath, the wrath will not last the entire seven years of the tribulation period.

Most people who hold this post-tribulational view do not make a clear distinction between God's program with the nation of Israel and the New Testament church. The church is the new Israel since Israel forfeited its right to be called the people of God by rejecting Jesus the Messiah. They see both the New Testament church and the nation of Israel on earth during the Great Tribulation period.

These are the main arguments used to support the post-tribulation rapture position. As we have emphasized with the other views, many godly Bible-believers embrace this position.

What Are Some Of The Major Objections And Biblical Problems With The Post-Tribulation Rapture Theory?

Post-Tribulationism believes the rapture of the church will take place at the very end of the seventieth week of Daniel or the great tribulation period. The living believers will be taken up in the clouds to meet the Lord and then, almost instantly, return with Him to enjoy His kingdom reign upon the earth.

While Post-Tribulationism has been the belief of many Christians down through the years there are a number of objections, as well as biblical problems, with this theory. They can be summarized as follows.

1. THERE ARE A NUMBER OF VARIATIONS OF POST-TRIBULATIONISM

There is one point in which all posttribulationists are in agreement. If there is a time of trouble just prior to the Second Coming of Jesus Christ, the church will need to pass through that difficult period. The one return of Christ to the earth brings deliverance from this period. Thus, the believers are not raptured before He returns. Consequently, the church will be raptured at the *end* of any tribulation period.

While posttribulationists are in agreement on this matter we find that this is where the agreements seemingly end. As we shall see, it is difficult to state a normative or standard view of Post-Tribulationism because of the variety of explanations which are given for each point in dispute.

For example, there is no agreement as to the doctrine of the tribulation. Is it a future time of wrath or is this divine wrath going on right now? If it is going on right now we may rightly ask when did is start? Was it at the beginning of the church age or does it go all the way back to Adam and Eve? Posttribulationists are divided over this. If the great tribulation is going on right now, then will there be an unprecedented time of trouble in the future? There is no consensus of agreement on this point either.

To sum up, a period of great trouble or tribulation cannot be unprecedented on the one hand and, at the same time, general throughout the church age. Either there will be a *specific* time of trouble or there will not be. There can be no meaningful discussion concerning the church going through the tribulation until there is some agreement on what is meant by the tribulation. Post-Tribulation does not give only one answer to this question.

Furthermore, there is no agreement among Post-Tribulationists as to whether the return of Jesus Christ will establish a literal thousand year period of peace upon the earth, the Millennium, or whether there will actually be a literal Millennium. We find posttribulationists who are amillenialists, those who reject a one thousand year earthly reign of Christ, as well as those which are premillennialists, the ones who believe there will be an earthly kingdom which lasts one thousand years after Christ returns.

In addition, there is no agreement as to what people will populate the kingdom when Christ returns. Will it be believers only, or will unbelievers also enter the kingdom? There is no consensus on this.

There is also a dispute over the types of bodies of those people who will enter the kingdom. Will they be human bodies, or glorified bodies, or both? Again, there is no consensus among Post-Tribulationists.

When will the judgment of the nations take place? Will it be at the return of Jesus Christ or at the end of the thousand-year Millennium?

Those who hold to Post-Tribulationism are not in agreement over this.

On these issues there is no agreement among those who hold to a post-tribulation rapture. In fact, a number of these views mutually exclude each other! Thus, they cannot be combined to come to a consensus view of the Post-Tribulation rapture doctrine. While this does not make the doctrine untrue, it does cause one to hesitate in calling this position "the standard view of the church."

2. IT IS WRONG TO CALL THIS THE HISTORIC VIEW

It is also wrong to label the Post-Tribulation rapture as the historic view of the church. For one thing, there was no unanimity of opinion among believers with respect to the timing of the rapture. In church history, the issue is either ignored or dealt with in the most cursory of ways. Many of the statements made by church leaders of the past are contradictory.

Actually, there was no attempt to provide a systematic understanding of this issue until the nineteenth century. Thus, there is certainly no consensus of opinion on the matter.

3. THE ISSUE OF THE NUMBER OF COMINGS OF CHRIST HAS TO BE DECIDED BY THE EVIDENCE

It is often argued that those who hold the Post-Tribulation view merely *assume* there is only one coming of Christ, which includes the rapture and the Second Coming, rather than proving it. In other words, they contend that the burden of proof is on those who see two different comings. There is no need *for them* to prove there is only one coming.

However, the Post-Tribulation view cannot win this point by default. It must show that the rapture and the Second Coming are one event by presenting a positive case. We should not start the debate by assuming the Post-Tribulation view is correct.

Furthermore, the fact that the same Greek words are used to describe both comings is irrelevant since we are not dealing with technical terms.

In addition, since the rapture and the Second Coming whether, one event or not, are both considered to be the "coming" of the Lord, it is not surprising to find the same words describing both.

The issue as to whether the rapture is a distinct coming of the Lord, which occurs at a different time than the Second Coming, has to be decided upon the evidence. The determination should not be made from the Greek words used to describe both events or by merely assuming the Post-Tribulation view is the correct one.

4. THE CHURCH IS WRONGLY IDENTIFIED WITH THE TRIBULATION SAINTS

Another criticism against the Post-Tribulation position is the identification of the New Testament church with the saints who are living through the great tribulation period. Nobody denies that there will be believers during this time. The question to be answered is the "identity" of these believers. While those who hold to Post-Tribulationism contend it is the church, there are others who reject this idea. They believe the reference to saints during this period is to "tribulation saints." These are people who have believed in Jesus Christ *after* the rapture has occurred. By misidentifying these people, Post-Tribulationism assumes that the church will remain through the entire period of tribulation.

5. POST-TRIBULATIONISM CONFUSES CONTEXTS

There is also the criticism that Post-Tribulationism confuses the contexts. In particular, we find this in the Olivet Discourse when Jesus spoke of His coming back to the earth. This is linked to such passages as First Thessalonians 4 and Second Thessalonians 2 which speak of the rapture. Jesus told believers to "watch;" Paul told believers to "watch." By linking these passages and emphasizing the things they have in common it is assumed they are speaking of the same event.

While there are certain things in common between Jesus' teaching of His return to the earth and Paul's explanation of the rapture, there are also many things that are distinct. These distinctions are not always appreciated.

The same holds true for the resurrection passages. The Bible often mentions several events together which do *not* occur at the same time. In the Old Testament, the prophets spoke of the two comings of Jesus Christ as one event. For example, the two comings of Christ are linked together in these two verses in Isaiah.

> For to us a child is born, to us a son is given, and the government will be on his shoulders. And he will be called Wonderful Counselor, Mighty God, Everlasting Father, Prince of Peace. Of the greatness of his government and peace there will be no end. He will reign on David's throne and over his kingdom, establishing and upholding it with justice and righteousness from that time on and forever. The zeal of the LORD Almighty will accomplish this (Isaiah 9:6-7)

Two thousand years have already separated Jesus' birth from His return to the earth. Since we find examples in Scripture of this type of telescoping of events we should not be surprised if we discover this to occur in passages dealing with the Lord's return.

In fact, we have a New Testament example of this. Jesus spoke of a time when the tombs will open and the dead will be raised.

> Do not be amazed at this, for a time is coming when all who are in their graves will hear his voice and come out--those who have done what is good will rise to live, and those who have done what is evil will rise to be condemned (John 5:28-29).

Yet this time when the believing dead and unbelieving dead are raised is later revealed to be one thousand years apart! We read.

> I saw thrones on which were seated those who had been
> given authority to judge. And I saw the souls of those who
> had been beheaded because of their testimony about Jesus
> and because of the word of God. They had not worshiped
> the beast or its image and had not received its mark on their
> foreheads or their hands. They came to life and reigned with
> Christ a thousand years. (The rest of the dead did not come
> to life until the thousand years were ended.) This is the first
> resurrection (Revelation 20:4-5).

Consequently, it is possible that the events listed in a particular passage do not all happen at the same time. Therefore, the verses which seemingly place the resurrection of Christians at the time of the Second Coming of Christ can be understood in another way.

THE BIBLE TEACHES THAT CHRIST CAN COME AT ANY MOMENT

Post-Tribulationism has to go against the clear New Testament teaching that the return of Jesus Christ is imminent. There was an expectation that Christ could come at any moment. We find no indication that believers were looking forward to persecution and tribulation before the coming of the Lord.

According to the Post-Tribulation position, the final Antichrist must come first as well as all the judgments listed in Revelation 6-18. The believer must be looking for these things before he or she looks for the coming of Christ.

Paul, however, wrote to Titus about our "blessed hope." He put it this way.

> While we wait for the blessed hope--the appearing of the
> glory of our great God and Savior, Jesus Christ (Titus 2:13).

The believers are to look for Jesus Christ, not the final Antichrist.

In addition, Paul wrote to the Philippians that he is eagerly awaiting the coming of the Savior.

> But our citizenship is in heaven. And we eagerly await a Savior from there, the Lord Jesus Christ, who, by the power that enables him to bring everything under his control, will transform our lowly bodies so that they will be like his glorious body (Philippians 3:20-21).

It is hard to see how the judgments recorded in Revelation 6-18 can be thought of as some type of "blessed hope." Furthermore, it is difficult to see how Paul can be earnestly awaiting the Savior if he first must experience the seven year period of persecution, possible martyrdom and then the wrath of God poured out upon the earth.

However, if the church is to go through the great tribulation period all of these things will be experienced before they see the blessed hope. Yet, this is not what we find the Christians looking for. Indeed, there is an "any moment" expectation of the return of Christ. This could not be true if the church had to go through the great tribulation period.

THERE IS AN INCORRECT DOCTRINE OF THE CHURCH

There is also the belief that those which hold the Post-Tribulation view have an incorrect doctrine of the church. The New Testament church, which is predominately Gentile, is not usually kept distinct from the nation of Israel in the Post-Tribulation scenario. We say, not usually, because there are some who hold the Post-Tribulation view which attempt to keep this distinction. However, they do not keep it consistently.

Scripture, however, *always* keeps the two distinct. The nation of Israel was specially selected by God to be the people through whom He would reach the world. When they rejected Jesus as their Messiah God temporarily set them aside. His work is now accomplished through the New Testament church which is made up of both Jews and Gentiles.

While the nation Israel has been set aside, this will not be forever. During the time of the great tribulation, or the seventieth week of Daniel, God will again deal with the nation Israel.

CONTRARY TO JESUS' STATEMENT THE EXACT DAY OF CHRIST'S COMING WOULD BE KNOWN

One problem recognized by those who hold to a Post-Tribulational rapture, as well as a literal millennial reign of Christ upon the earth, concerns the knowledge of when the rapture/Second Coming would take place. Careful students of Bible prophecy recognize that the seventieth week of Daniel starts with a signing or the confirming of an agreement between the coming leader of a revived Roman empire, known as the "man of sin," and the nation of Israel (Daniel 9:27).

Exactly three and one half years into the seven year agreement the pact with Israel is broken. Three and one half years later, Jesus Christ returns. The problem with this scenario is that Jesus said *nobody* knows the day or hour of His return.

> But about that day or hour no one knows, not even the angels in heaven, nor the Son, but only the Father (Matthew 24:36).

Yet it seems for those who insist that the rapture takes place at the same time as the Second Coming the day could be calculated. It would be exactly seven years from the time of the signing of the agreement or three and a half years after the treaty is broken. Thus, it contradicts the words of Jesus that nobody can know the day or hour of His coming.

This problem has been recognized by some who hold the Post-Tribulation view. In response, they usually insert some short interval between the time of the rapture and the Second Coming. However, when one does this they have acknowledged an interval of time is necessary between these two events. If an interval must exist, then why can't it be three and half years or seven years? It seems that once someone admits there must be some interval of time, no matter how short, between the rapture and the Second Coming the Post-Tribulation explanation must be abandoned.

THERE IS AN INCORRECT VIEW OF THE SEVENTIETH WEEK OF DANIEL (THE NATURE OF THE TRIBULATION)

Post-Tribulationism is criticized for having an incorrect view of the seventieth week of Daniel. The last seven years are a time when the Lord deals with *Israel* as a nation as He did during the Old Testament period. Indeed, the angel Gabriel made it clear that it was the future of *Daniel's people* which was in view.

> Seventy 'sevens' are decreed for your people and your holy city (Daniel 9:24)

"Your people" is Israel while "your holy city" is Jerusalem.

We are now in an interval between the sixty-ninth and seventieth week of Daniel, the church age. Once the church age ends, then the Lord will again deal with Israel. This is crucial to understand.

Since God's dealings will be mainly through Israel at this time, it is not necessary for the New Testament church, the Christians, to exist on the earth. This is why many believe the rapture will take place *before* the seventieth week of Daniel. We can make the following observations.

THE GREAT TRIBULATION

The time of trouble referred to by Christ as the "great tribulation" was to have such a specific character as to make it a sign of the His approaching Second Coming. In fact, Jesus said that the great tribulation was one of the signs of the end of the age. The disciples asked the Lord about the "sign" of His coming.

> As Jesus was sitting on the Mount of Olives, the disciples came to him privately. "Tell us," they said, "when will this

happen, and what will be the sign of your coming and of the
end of the age?" (Matthew 24:3).

The phrase "great tribulation" or "great distress" actually comes from
Jesus Himself as He describes this future period. We read the following
in Matthew.

For then there will be great distress, unequaled from the beginning of
the world until now--and never to be equaled again (Matthew 24:21).

The Old Testament speaks of this future time. It is called the "time of
Jacob's trouble" or "distress for Jacob." The following is recorded in the
Book of Jeremiah.

> How awful that day will be! No other will be like it. It will
> be a time of trouble for Jacob, but he will be saved out of it
> (Jeremiah 30:7).

The Book of Daniel also speaks of this period. We read the following.

> At that time Michael, the great prince who protects your
> people, will arise. There will be a time of distress such as
> has not happened from the beginning of nations until then.
> But at that time your people--everyone whose name is found
> written in the book--will be delivered (Daniel 12:1).

Post-Tribulationism has no single answer to this issue of the great distress, or the seventieth week of Daniel. As mentioned, some see it as the
entire period from Jesus Christ until the present. Others actually see
the time of wrath as something which goes back all the way to Adam.
Still others see it as a distinct period of unprecedented trouble which is
yet future. Yet, if it is a distinct period, there must be some explanation
as to *why* it is different. It is consistent, therefore, to see the church
removed during this specific period when the Lord once again deals
with the nation of Israel.

10. THE WRATH OF GOD IS POURED OUT DURING THE ENTIRE SEVENTIETH WEEK OF DANIEL

The Post-Tribulation position holds that the wrath of God is not poured out during the entire seventieth week of Daniel. Instead, it is limited to the very end of the seven year period.

Yet we find the wrath of God occurring at the very beginning of the seventieth week of Daniel. Indeed, with the opening of the first seal we read the following judgment.

> I watched as the Lamb opened the first of the seven seals. Then I heard one of the four living creatures say in a voice like thunder, "Come!" I looked, and there before me was a white horse! Its rider held a bow, and he was given a crown, and he rode out as a conqueror bent on conquest (Revelation 6:1-2).

While this intensifies as the time of the Second Coming draws closer, it is wrong to say that it does not occur until the very end of this seven-year period. If the entire seventieth week of Daniel is a time of God's wrath being poured out upon the earth then we would expect the church to be removed during this specific period of judgment.

11. THE LAST TRUMPET OF FIRST CORINTHIANS IS NOT THE SAME AS THE TRUMPET JUDGMENTS

While the trumpet reference in First Corinthians is often equated with the last of the trumpet judgments in the Book of Revelation there are some problems with this view.

For one thing, the Book of Revelation had not even been written when Paul wrote this to the Corinthians! Therefore, it seems unlikely that Paul's audience would understand the last trumpet to be equated with future trumpet judgments which had not been revealed yet.

In addition, the trumpet blasts in Revelation are calls to *judgment*. The sound of the trumpet in Corinthians is a call to meet the Lord. Indeed, it is a joyful sound, not something to be dreaded. This trumpet signifies that the dead in Christ as well as the living believers will be given a glorified body. This allows them to enter into the presence of Jesus Christ.

SO WHAT IS THE LAST TRUMPET IN FIRST CORINTHIANS?

What does the "last trumpet" refer to? There are a number of possibilities. The trumpet analogy in First Corinthians may be connected with the practice of the Roman army. Three trumpets would blow. The first trumpet caused the army to break up the camp. The second trumpet would have them line up in marching formation. The last trumpet was a call to depart. This last trumpet analogy would fit with that which Paul wrote to the Corinthians. The believers in Jesus Christ are now prepared to leave this world. In doing so, they are presently waiting to hear the last trumpet which would indicate that it is time for them to depart.

There is also the possibility that the "last trumpet" may be a unique trumpet which sounds for the church at the rapture. In fact, there are possibly two trumpet blasts. The first one is for the dead, which will rise first, and then a second or last trumpet for the living. Thus, the living believers are caught away at the sound of the second trumpet.

Whatever the case may be it is not necessary to link the trumpet judgments in Revelation with the trumpet which blows at the time of the rapture.

12. THERE IS NO ADEQUATE EXPLANATION AS TO WHO WILL POPULATE THE MILLENNIUM

This is probably the biggest problem for those which hold to the Post-Tribulation view; their explanation of who will populate the Millennium. While this is not a problem for those who do not believe there will be a literal Millennium here upon the earth, amillenialists, or those which believe that Christ will return after the Millennium, post-millennialists, there are many people who hold the Post-Tribulation view who believe Christ will come before the Millennium. They are the pre-millennialists. They have no satisfactory explanation as to who will populate the Millennium.

THE PROBLEM STATED

We can simply state the problem in the following manner. If there will be a literal thousand year period of peace on earth when Jesus Christ returns, then someone has to populate the earth at that time. According to many promises in the Old Testament there will be both Jews and Gentiles living together during that period. These people live in the same type of bodies we have now; non-glorified human bodies.

Though the curse on the earth will be partially lifted, people will still sin, and they will one day die. They have not received glorified bodies like the believers who receive these bodies at the rapture of the church. There are a number of passages that make it clear.

PEOPLE WILL BE CAPABLE OF SINNING DURING THE MILLENNIUM

To begin with, we find that there will be children born in the Millennium and these children will be capable of sin.

We read in Isaiah.

> Never again will there be in it an infant who lives but a few days, or an old man who does not live out his years; the one who dies at a hundred will be thought a mere child; the one who fails to reach a hundred will be considered accursed (Isaiah 65:20).

Thus, Scripture emphasizes that people still sin during this period. Indeed, the Bible says that at the end of the thousand years there will be rebellion against the Lord from many of those living on the earth.

> When the thousand years are over, Satan will be released from his prison and will go out to deceive the nations in the

four corners of the earth--Gog and Magog--and to gather
them for battle. In number they are like the sand on the
seashore (Revelation 20:7-8)

This certainly describes people in a *non-glorified* human body since
a glorified body of the believer can neither sin nor can it die. Where
do these unbelievers come from? They are the offspring of those who
entered the thousand year period as believers. They will make their own
choice as to whether they will follow Jesus.

All of this means that someone has to enter the millennial kingdom
in sinful non-glorified bodies. However, if the rapture of the church
occurs immediately before Christ returns, then, by definition, *all*
believers have received their new bodies. The only people who have not
been transformed are the unbelievers. So we are left with believers in
new bodies and unbelievers in their old bodies.

THERE WILL BE A SEPARATION OF BELIEVERS AND UNBELIEVERS

Furthermore, the Bible teaches that the unbelievers will be separated
from the believers at the time of the Second Coming of Christ. When
the Lord judges the nations upon His return He separates the sheep
from the goats, the believers from the unbelievers. Only believers will
enter the kingdom. Jesus said.

> When the Son of Man comes in his glory, and all the angels
> with him, he will sit on his glorious throne. All the nations
> will be gathered before him, and he will separate the people
> one from another as a shepherd separates the sheep from the
> goats. He will put the sheep on his right and the goats on his
> left (Matthew 25:31-33).

But here is the problem for the Post-Tribulational position. Who are
these believers with non-glorified bodies who will enter the kingdom?
All of the righteous have glorified bodies. Where do these other righteous people come from? Moreover, if only righteous people in glorified

bodies enter the kingdom then who are the people that sin, grow old, and die?

To many, this difficulty renders the Post-Tribulational, pre-millennial view as impossible because there is no reasonable answer which they have to this question.

THERE IS NO ADEQUATE EXPLANATION FOR THE RAPTURE

Post-Tribulationism has never really given an adequate explanation as to why there is such an event as the rapture of the church. In their scenario, Christ takes the living and dead believers to meet Him in the air on His way down to the earth. It seems so unnecessary. Why would the Lord miraculously preserve many of the true believers through the entire tribulation period only to take them up to meet Him on His way to the earth?

Then there is the issue of raising the dead believers. Why raise them at this time? They are certainly not in jeopardy from the battles being waged at Armageddon. A rapture which takes place at this particular time does not seem to make any sense.

If the rapture is mainly to meet the Lord as He returns to the earth, then there are other problems. The judgment of the nations which Jesus spoke of has no real meaning. In this judgment, the King separates the sheep from the goats; the believers from the unbelievers. However, if the rapture of the saints has just happened then the separation has *already* occurred! There would be no need to separate the saved from the lost because this has just been accomplished. Therefore, the rapture seems so unnecessary in the Post-Tribulational view of the coming of Christ.

THERE ARE NO ADEQUATE ANSWERS TO THESE OBJECTIONS

To sum up, it appears that the Post-Tribulation position does not have adequate answers to these and other objections. While at first this theory may seem like the best way to understand the coming of Jesus Christ, the more one looks at the Scripture the less convincing the arguments become. Therefore, for many who have looked deeply into the issue of the rapture of the church the Post-Tribulation answer has not been convincing.

SUMMARY TO QUESTION 17
WHAT ARE SOME OF THE MAJOR OBJECTIONS AND BIBLICAL PROBLEMS WITH THE POST-TRIBULATION RAPTURE THEORY?

The post-tribulation rapture theory says that the New Testament church, the true believers in Jesus, will not be removed from the earth by means of the rapture of the church until the time when Christ returns. There is no escape for Christians for any of the predicted judgments found in the Book of Revelation. The believers will be caught up to meet Jesus in the air while He is on His way to the earth. Post-tribulation, thus, rejects all theories which claim there is an interval between the time of the catching up of the church, the rapture, and the Second Coming of Christ.

While the post-tribulation theory has been very popular among Bible-believing Christians there are a number of objections to it. We can list the main ones as follows.

One problem is defining the post-tribulation rapture position. This is not entirely easy to do. While all post-tribulation adherents believe the coming of Christ is one complex event, with the rapture as part of that event, there are many things in which they disagree among themselves.

For example, those who hold this position do not agree on the nature of the Great Tribulation or if there even is such a period. They do not agree as to whether Christ will come back to set up a literal kingdom upon the earth, a millennium, or whether there is such a thing as a literal thousand year earthly reign of Christ when He returns. In addition, there is no agreement as to when Christ will judge the nations.

There is no agreement as to whom, if anyone, will populate the earth when Christ comes back.

Furthermore, it is wrong to call the post-tribulation rapture the historic view of the church. For one thing, the issue of the rapture was hardly dealt with until recently in the church. The ones who did deal with it in the past often gave contradictory answers. It was not until the end of the nineteenth century when this issue began to be seriously debated. The real question is discovering what the Bible says about this matter; not who supposedly has the oldest view.

Everyone agrees there will be believers during the future time of tribulation. Those holding to the post-tribulation rapture are said to be misidentifying the believers in this seven year period. While they assume the elect, or the saints, refers to the church, there is stronger evidence that the believers are actually the tribulation saints; those who believe in Jesus after the rapture has taken place. Thus, they are not part of this special group of believers known as the church.

Post-tribulationism is also accused of confusion of contexts. They link Jesus' statements in Matthew 24-25 with Paul's statement in First and Second Thessalonians. While the subject is the coming of Christ in both contexts, it has to be established that both are not talking about the same coming. The descriptions are different enough to provide sufficient evidence to believe in two comings; one for believers and another with the believers to set up the kingdom. Many accuse post-tribulationism of being in error in denying the imminent or "any moment" coming of Christ. Instead of looking for Jesus, those who hold the post-tribulation view must be looking for antichrist and the judgments of Revelation 6-18. There is no "any moment" coming of the Lord.

The post-tribulation advocates are also accused of confusion as to the identity of Israel and the New Testament church. Unless one understands the distinct programs which God has for Israel and the church, then they will not be able to interpret end-time events in a consistent manner.

The nature of the Great Tribulation, the seventieth week of Daniel, is also said to be confused by those holding the Post-tribulation perspective. This is a specific time God will deal with the nation of Israel. It completes the last seven year period in which God is specifically dealing with Israel before the Messiah, Jesus Christ, returns.

There is also a huge problem for those which hold a premillennial coming of Christ as well as a post-tribulation rapture; who will populate the millennium? If everyone is taken up in the rapture at the Second Coming of Christ then nobody is left to populate the earth in mortal bodies for the coming kingdom. There has never been a satisfactory answer given to this question. There has never been a good explanation from post-tribulationism as to why there is such a thing as the rapture. Why would the Lord catch the believers in the air only to turn them around and come to earth again? Why then separate the sheep from the goats at the judgment when the rapture has just separated them? It does not make any sense.

It seems that no adequate explanation can be given for all of these objections. Thus, we conclude that there are just too many problems with the post-tribulation position. This has caused many to seek a better explanation as to the timing of the rapture.

QUESTION 18

What Is The Pre-Tribulation Rapture View?

Thus far we have looked at a number of views concerning the rapture of the church. As we have noted, each one seems to have insurmountable problems. While there are good Bible-believing people who hold each of these views none of them seems to be the correct way of understanding the question of the timing of the rapture of the church.

However, we believe that there is one approach to this question that does give satisfactory answers to this question. This is the doctrine of Pre-tribulationism, or the Pre-Trib rapture view.

THE PRE-TRIB VIEW DEFINED

The Pretribulational, or Pre-Trib, position sees a future seven-year period, known as the seventieth week of Daniel or the great tribulation, which will occur upon the earth. It will be a time of unprecedented trouble. However, believers in Jesus Christ will escape this entire period by being supernaturally caught up to meet the Lord in the air; the rapture of the church.

These living believers will be transformed immediately after the "dead in Christ" are first raised to meet Jesus in the air. The Lord Himself will then bring these believers back to heaven into the presence of God the Father. At that time, they will receive their individual rewards for service.

After the rapture of the church takes place, the seven-year "seventieth week of Daniel" begins on the earth with all its predicted judgments. At the end of the seven years, Jesus Christ returns to the world with His saints to set up His earthly kingdom.

He then rules and reigns on the earth for one thousand years, the Millennium. After the thousand years is over there is a final judgment of unbelievers. Then His eternal rule begins!

This is a brief summation of the Pre-Tribulation rapture position and some of the events associated with it. We now list the following points in favor of the Pre-Tribulation rapture.

THERE IS CONSISTENT LITERAL INTERPRETATION OF SCRIPTURE

One of the pillars of the Pre-Tribulation viewpoint is the consistent literal method of interpretation of Scripture. Simply put, all of Scripture, including the prophetic portions, is to be interpreted in a normal and plain way. When the Bible is interpreted in a literal manner then a Pre-Tribulation rapture will be the result. Thus, literal interpretation is foundational to the Pre-Trib viewpoint.

2. THERE IS CLEAR EVIDENCE IN SCRIPTURE OF TWO COMINGS OF CHRIST

The Bible speaks of the coming again of Jesus Christ. Those who hold to the Pre-Tribulation position must be able to show from Scripture that the rapture and the Second Coming are dissimilar enough for them to be two distinct events separated by time. Those who hold this view believe this is something which can be done.

Indeed, it is contended when all the facts are in, the details concerning the coming of Christ *cannot* be properly explained if we assume only one coming at the end of the seventieth week of Daniel, the great tribulation.

When passages are examined which clearly teach the rapture, and compared with other passages which clearly speak of the Second Coming, it can be shown that there is sufficient reason to believe these passages are talking about *two* different events which do not happen at the same time. If this is the case, then it takes away one of the favorite arguments of the posttribulationists; there is only one coming of Christ.

Two future comings of Christ, one for believers in the rapture, and another seven years later to set up His kingdom, can be consistently upheld when one looks at *all* of the evidence.

We will now present some of the contrasts between the two events.

A. THE DESTINATIONS ARE DIFFERENT

When Jesus Christ comes for believers at the rapture He takes them back to His Father's house in heaven. However, at the Second Coming the Lord brings the saints with Him as He comes to the earth to rule as King. Thus, the destinations of the comings of Christ are different. At the rapture they go to the house of the Father while at the Second Coming the destination is earth.

CHRIST GATHERS HIS BELIEVERS AT THE RAPTURE, THE ANGELS GATHER THE ELECT AT THE SECOND COMING

When the rapture occurs it is Jesus Christ who gathers His own. We read the following.

> For the Lord himself will come down from heaven, with a loud command, with the voice of the archangel and with the trumpet call of God, and the dead in Christ will rise first (1 Thessalonians 4:16).

However, at the Second Coming of Christ it is the angels who gather the elect. Matthew wrote.

> Then will appear the sign of the Son of Man in heaven. And then all the peoples of the earth will mourn when they see the Son of Man coming on the clouds of heaven, with power and

great glory. And he will send his angels with a loud trumpet call, and they will gather his elect from the four winds, from one end of the heavens to the other (Matthew 24:30-31).

Thus, there is a distinction as to who gathers the believers; it is Jesus Himself at the rapture but we find that angels gather the saints at the Second Coming.

C. THE RAPTURE IS A TIME OF REWARD, THE SECOND COMING A TIME OF JUDGMENT

Jesus gathers His church at the rapture for the purpose of *rewarding* them. The judgment seat of Christ is a time of rewarding believers for deeds done for Him. Paul wrote.

> For we must all appear before the judgment seat of Christ, so that each of us may receive what is due us for the things done while in the body, whether good or bad. (2 Corinthians 5:10)

However, at the Second Coming the Lord Jesus returns to judge, not reward, those living upon the earth. Jesus said.

> When the Son of Man comes in his glory, and all the angels with him, he will sit on his glorious throne. All the nations will be gathered before him, and he will separate the people one from another as a shepherd separates the sheep from the goats (Matthew 25:31-32).

Again we find a different purpose for the two comings.

D. THE RAPTURE IS NEVER MENTIONED IN PASSAGES PICTURING THE SECOND COMING OF CHRIST

There is something else that is important to note. In every passage which mentions the actual Second Coming of Christ to the earth we never find the rapture of the church clearly mentioned. While this does not, of itself, prove the rapture of the church and the Second Coming of Christ are two distinct events, it is noteworthy that this is what we find.

THESE DIFFERENCES REVEAL TWO DISTINCT EVENTS

We believe these differences give strong evidence that the rapture of the church and the Second Coming of Christ to the earth are two distinct events separated by an interval of time. As we have noted, this time interval lasts seven years.

3. THE CHURCH IS NEVER FOUND IN PASSAGES DEALING WITH THE TRIBULATION

Another strong argument for the Pre-Tribulation rapture has to do with the absence of the church on earth during the description of the great tribulation. The church is mentioned some nineteen times in the first three chapters of the Book of Revelation. However, from chapter four through chapter nineteen, when the subject is the great tribulation or the wrath of God coming upon the earth, the church on the earth is not mentioned at all. In fact, the only other time the church is mentioned on the earth is at the end of the last chapter of the Book of Revelation (22:16). This takes place after the Lord has returned and has created a new heaven and a new earth.

Why, it is asked, would John give detailed instructions to the church in the first three chapters and then entirely ignore the church on earth in the rest of the Book of Revelation? This question is especially significant since these chapters deal with the darkest period of earth's history, the great tribulation.

Why are there no warnings to the church concerning how they are to prepare for this period? The best answer to this question is that the church is no longer on the earth. Indeed, they have been caught up to meet the Lord in the air and thus will not experience the great tribulation period.

ISRAEL IS HIGHLIGHTED DURING THE GREAT TRIBULATION PERIOD

While we do not find passages that show the church is on earth during the great tribulation, we do find passages where the nation Israel exists during this time. Indeed, there are passages in Revelation chapter seven and chapter fourteen where 144,000 people from the nation of Israel are sealed as God's witnesses during this period.

We also find Israel highlighted in Revelation chapter twelve in the account of the woman who gave birth to the male child. This chapter actually gives a summary of the entire tribulation period. The focus of this section is on the nation Israel.

Question: Why do we find this emphasis if the church is still existing on the earth? Why is there no mention of them being persecuted seeing that it is a time of persecution toward those who believe in the God of the Bible? Thus, the switch from the church, in the first three chapters, to Israel in the remaining chapters, is significant.

One last thing should be noted. We never find in Scripture the church and Israel existing at the same time as the particular people through whom God is reaching the world with His message. It is either Israel or the church; it is never Israel and the church!

The fact that Israel is highlighted in these chapters and the church is not mentioned seemingly makes it clear that the church age is over once the great tribulation begins. The Lord now resumes His dealings with the nation of Israel.

5. IT IS NOT NECESSARY FOR THE CHURCH TO EXIST DURING THE TRIBULATION

The reason we do not find the church on earth during the great tribulation period is because it is not necessary for it to be there. The preaching of Jesus Christ will occur apart from those in the New Testament church. Indeed, we are told of three powerful sources of testimony to the message of Christ during the great tribulation period.

THE 144,000

First, there are the 144,000. We are introduced to them in the Book of Revelation by an angel who said the following words to four other angels who were about to harm the land and the sea.

> Do not harm the land or the sea or the trees until we put a seal on the foreheads of the servants of our God. Then I heard the number of those who were sealed: 144,000 from all the tribes of Israel (Revelation 7:3-4).

These 144,000 are supernaturally protected by the Lord through this period of tribulation. Clearly, the reason for their protection is to spread the gospel. Later we read the following about them.

> Then I looked, and there before me was the Lamb, standing on Mount Zion, and with him 144,000 who had his name and his Father's name written on their foreheads. And I heard a sound from heaven like the roar of rushing waters and like a loud peal of thunder. The sound I heard was like that of harpists playing their harps. And they sang a new song before the throne and before the four living creatures and the elders. No one could learn the song except the 144,000 who had been redeemed from the earth (Revelation 14:1-3).

These special witnesses will evidently give testimony about Jesus during this period of tribulation.

THE TWO WITNESSES

Next we have the ministry of the two witnesses. They are described as having the following ministry during the time of tribulation.

> And I will appoint my two witnesses, and they will prophesy for 1,260 days, clothed in sackcloth. They are "the two olive trees" and the two lampstands, and "they stand before the Lord of the earth." If anyone tries to harm them, fire comes

from their mouths and devours their enemies. This is how anyone who wants to harm them must die. They have power to shut up the heavens so that it will not rain during the time they are prophesying; and they have power to turn the waters into blood and to strike the earth with every kind of plague as often as they want (Revelation 11:3-6).

Their testimony is to everyone on the earth.

THE ANGEL WITH THE EVERLASTING GOSPEL

Finally, we are told of an angel who preaches an everlasting gospel.

Then I saw another angel flying in midair, and he had the eternal gospel to proclaim to those who live on the earth--to every nation, tribe, language and people (Revelation 14:6).

Between the 144,000 from Israel, the two witnesses, and the angel preaching the everlasting gospel to the entire world, the message of Jesus Christ will blanket the earth during the time of the great tribulation. The church is not on earth during these seven years neither is it needed.

6. THE KEY RAPTURE PASSAGE (1 THESSALONIANS 4:13-18) MAKES IT CLEAR THE RAPTURE IS PRE-TRIBULATIONAL

An examination of the key passage on the rapture of the church, 1 Thessalonians 4:13-18, shows that the Thessalonians were expecting a Pre-Tribulation rapture.

Paul wrote this section because the Thessalonians were worried about their departed love ones. It seems that they were concerned that these dead believers would miss the rapture of the church. This assumes a Pre-Tribulation rapture. Why? If the rapture were at the end of the tribulation period then there would be no need to worry about these dead believers since they would not have to face the coming wrath. In fact, we would expect the Thessalonians to be happy that their dead loved ones would escape the coming great tribulation. Instead we find the Thessalonians worried about these departed saints.

The fact that the Thessalonians were concerned about their departed loved ones instead of themselves indicates they were not personally worried about the wrath of God which was going to come upon the earth. The lack of concern for their own future seems to show that Paul already assured them that the church would *not* be around for that particular period of trouble.

Moreover, we do not find Paul instructing them about how to deal with the coming wrath. Instead he tells them of the wonderful event which will occur that will remove them from the earth *before* that time of trouble, the rapture of the church.

Again, if these Thessalonians were expecting to experience the great tribulation it is inconceivable that they did not ask any questions about how they should behave during this period. Furthermore, at the very least, we should expect Paul to warn them. However, neither of these things happened. The simplest explanation is that they were not expecting to endure such a period of trouble because the Lord would remove them from the earth before He poured out His mighty wrath.

7. THE BLESSED HOPE IS LOOKING FOR CHRIST NOT ANTICHRIST OR THE JUDGMENTS OF REVELATION 6-19

The believers have a blessed hope in the return of Jesus Christ for those who have trusted in Him. Paul wrote.

> While we wait for the blessed hope--the appearing of the glory of our great God and Savior, Jesus Christ (Titus 2:13).

However, if the Pre-Tribulation rapture doctrine is not true then we are not looking for Christ first but rather Antichrist. All of the judgments of the great tribulation, clearly spelled out in Revelation 6-18, have to take place *before* believers can look for the coming of Christ. This does not seem to be much of a "blessed hope" for the believer!

8. THE CHURCH IS NOT SUBJECT TO GOD'S WRATH

The Bible clearly says that God has not appointed New Testament believers to wrath. Paul began his letter to the Thessalonians encouraging them that they would be rescued from the coming wrath.

> And to wait for his Son from heaven, whom he raised from the dead--Jesus, who rescues us from the coming wrath (1 Thessalonians 1:10).

This is not only speaking of the future wrath of "hell" or the "lake of fire," it is also speaking of the coming wrath, the great tribulation, which those on earth will experience.

He emphasized this again when he wrote.

> For God did not appoint us to suffer wrath but to receive salvation through our Lord Jesus Christ (1 Thessalonians 5:9).

This verse is clear. God's people in this age, the church, are not appointed to wrath. In fact, the entire context of this verse emphasizes this fact. If the great tribulation is a time of wrath, then believers in Jesus Christ certainly should be provided a way of escape. According to the Pre-Tribulation rapture position they are provided this escape through the "catching up" of the church.

THE TRIBULATION SAINTS ARE NOT THE CHURCH

There are people who become believers during the great tribulation *after* the church is raptured. However, they are not considered to be part of the New Testament church. They are known as the "tribulation saints." These individuals will be on the earth when the wrath of God strikes. Because they had rejected the message of Christ, they will miss the rapture. However, God, in His grace, will allow them to be saved after the church is gone. Yet, they will have to be on the earth when the terrible judgments come. As to whether some of them will be supernaturally protected from the coming judgments is an issue that is debated.

This is a topic that most prophecy teachers agree upon; that the Christians will not be subject to the wrath of God. However, what they do not agree upon is exactly "when" the wrath of God begins with respect to the judgments recorded in the Book of Revelation. The Pre-Tribulation position is that the entire seventieth week of Daniel, or the great tribulation period, is a time of God's wrath upon the unbelieving world. If that can be demonstrated, then the Pre-Tribulation rapture seems to be a necessity.

9. THERE ARE NO WARNINGS TO PREPARE BELIEVERS FOR THE GREAT TRIBULATION

If Christians must experience some or all of the seventieth week of Daniel, the great tribulation period, then why don't we find *any* specific warning about it in Scripture? This is a bit strange because the New Testament believers are warned about a number of things which they would experience. We can cite the following examples.

A. BELIEVERS ARE WARNED ABOUT FALSE PROPHETS

We find believers are warned about false prophets. The Apostle Paul had the following words to say to the elders of Ephesus about these individuals.

> I know that after I leave, savage wolves will come in among you and will not spare the flock (Acts 20:29).

Peter also wrote warned about the false teachers among the people. He put it this way.

> But there were also false prophets among the people, just as there will be false teachers among you. They will secretly

introduce destructive heresies, even denying the sovereign Lord who bought them--bringing swift destruction on themselves (2 Peter 2:1).

Christians had to be aware that false prophets and false teachers were in their midst. These false prophets were a genuine threat to their spiritual well-being. Consequently, they were warned.

B. CHRISTIANS ARE WARNED ABOUT UNGODLY LIVING

Christians are also warned about living in an ungodly manner. For example, the writer to the Hebrews said.

> Therefore, since we are surrounded by such a great cloud of witnesses, let us throw off everything that hinders and the sin that so easily entangles. And let us run with perseverance the race marked out for us (Hebrews 12:1).

It was important for the biblical writers to give believers this particular warning.

C. CHRISTIANS ARE WARNED ABOUT PRESENT TRIALS AND TRIBULATIONS

Believers are warned about the present trouble or tribulation they were experiencing. Paul wrote to the Thessalonians.

> Therefore, among God's churches we boast about your per-severance and faith in all the persecutions and trials you are enduring (2 Thessalonians 1:4).

Earlier, he said this to the church at Thessalonica.

> And we also thank God continually because, when you received the word of God, which you heard from us, you accepted it not as a human word, but as it actually is, the word of God, which is indeed at work in you who believe. For you, brothers and sisters, became imitators of God's

churches in Judea, which are in Christ Jesus: You suffered from your own people the same things those churches suffered from the Jews (1 Thessalonians 2:13-14).

Christians were being warned about the present troubles they were facing. Indeed, we find that the entire Book of First Peter contains warning about present problems and persecution.

WHY NO WARNINGS ABOUT THE GREAT TRIBULATION?

Yet with all of these warnings in Scripture, we find *no* specific warnings about how to deal with the coming great tribulation. There is total silence from the Bible on this issue. This is unimaginable if the church would be on earth going through this time. The greatest time of trouble which the people on the earth will ever experience is not even mentioned. Nothing is said about what to do when this period occurs, how long they will have to endure it, or the purpose of these believers experiencing this unprecedented period. Why?

The simple answer as to why there are no warnings for the church about how to survive during this dreadful period is because the church is *not* going to be around during this time. The Lord will remove them from the world.

THERE MUST BE SUFFICIENT TIME FOR CERTAIN EVENTS TO OCCUR BEFORE CHRIST COMES

The Pre-Tribulation view of the rapture of the church says that there is a seven-year interval between the catching up of the Christians and the Second Coming of Jesus Christ to the earth. In other words, they are two distinct events which do not happen at the same time.

There are many reasons for believing such an interval is necessary. One reason concerns two specific events which must take place *after* the rapture but *before* the Second Coming. These important events are the Judgment Seat of Christ and the Marriage of the Lamb. We can make the following observations.

THE BRIDE AND GROOM MUST MARRY

The Bible says that there will be a marriage between Jesus, the groom, and His bride, the church. Nobody doubts this. We know that the church is the "bride of Christ." The Apostle Paul wrote.

> I am jealous for you with a godly jealousy. I promised you to one husband, to Christ, so that I might present you as a pure virgin to him (2 Corinthians 11:2).

The church is compared to a virgin bride.

Paul wrote to the Ephesians.

> For this reason a man will leave his father and mother and be united to his wife, and the two will become one flesh. This is a profound mystery--but I am talking about Christ and the church (Ephesians 5:31-32)

Again, the church is compared to a bride.

THE RETURN OF JESUS WITH THE HEAVENLY ARMY

When Jesus Christ comes back to the earth after the great tribulation He will be joined by a heavenly army. The Bible puts it this way.

> Let us rejoice and be glad and give him glory! For the wedding of the Lamb has come, and his bride has made herself ready. Fine linen, bright and clean, was given her to wear (Fine linen stands for the righteous acts of God's holy people.) Then the angel said to me, "Write this: Blessed are those who are invited to the wedding supper of the Lamb!" And he added, "These are the true words of God.". . . The armies of heaven were following him, riding on white horses and dressed in fine linen, white and clean (Revelation 19:7–9,14)

The fine linen the saints are wearing identifies them as the "wife" of the Lamb. They return with Christ as He comes back to make war against those remaining on the earth. The return of the Lord with His bride helps us in our understanding of the timing of the rapture.

THE MARRIAGE OF THE LAMB HAS TAKEN PLACE IN HEAVEN

The fact that the Lord is returning *with* His bride shows that she has made herself ready *before* He comes to the earth. At the time of Jesus' return to the earth the actual marriage between the bride and the groom has already taken place.

Notice that the Bible says the bride is wearing fine linen bright and clean. She has readied herself for the marriage supper or marriage feast. This is the *celebration* of the wedding. The invitations are about to go out, the marriage feast is about to begin. The groom brings the bride with Him and the guests will join the celebration.

It is when Jesus Christ returns to the earth that the marriage feast takes place; the celebration of that wedding. This feast is described for us in Matthew 25:1-13. However, to have a celebration of the wedding you must first have the wedding. When did this happen? Obviously it was at some previous time.

Consequently, for the wife to be ready, she must have been with the Lord in heaven. This assumes that she had been taken there at an earlier time. What time was that? It was at the rapture of the church.

THE JUDGMENT SEAT OF CHRIST TAKES PLACE IN HEAVEN

There is something else which must take place. Scripture speaks of an event called "the judgment seat of Christ." This is where Christ gives rewards to believers. Paul wrote the following to the Corinthians.

> For we must all appear before the judgment seat of Christ, so that each of us may receive what is due us for the things done while in the body, whether good or bad (2 Corinthians 5:10).

In another place, Paul described it in more detail. He wrote.

> By the grace God has given me, I laid a foundation as a wise builder, and someone else is building on it. But each one should build with care. For no one can lay any foundation other than the one already laid, which is Jesus Christ. If anyone builds on this foundation using gold, silver, costly stones, wood, hay or straw their work will be shown for what it is, because the Day will bring it to light. It will be revealed with fire, and the fire will test the quality of each person's work. If what has been built survives, the builder will receive a reward. If it is burned up, the builder will suffer loss but yet will be saved--even though only as one escaping through the flames (1 Corinthians 3:10-15).

According to these passages, believers of this age must appear before the judgment seat of Christ. At this event there will be an evaluation of our works and then rewards will be given for faithful service.

When the Lord returns with His church this evaluation has already occurred and these rewards have already been given out. The Bible says.

> Fine linen, bright and clean, was given her to wear. (Fine linen stands for the righteous acts of God's holy people.) (Revelation 19:8)

It is clear that the rewards have *already* been given out because the wedding garments are embroidered with the righteous deeds of the saints. The judgment seat of Christ has already taken place. An evaluation of this type would, of necessity, take some time. It is hardly possible to see how this could occur if the rapture took place at the same time as the Second Coming of Christ.

THE IMPLICATIONS FOR THE TIMING OF THE RAPTURE

The implications are seemingly obvious. The church, the New Testament Christians, must spend some time in heaven with the Lord before they return to earth together. The fact that the church is now the wife of the Lamb, and each believer has been rewarded for his or her individual deeds necessitates an interval of time. There is certainly no reason to believe that these two marvelous events take place in a split second.

Thus, an interval between the rapture of the church and the Second Coming of Christ is necessary. This fits well with the Pre-Tribulation view of the rapture which has the church saints in heaven during the time of the great tribulation on the earth.

11. A COMPARISON BETWEEN JOHN 14:1-3 AND 1 THESSALONIANS 4:13-18 SHOWS THE RAPTURE MUST BE PRE-TRIBULATION

A comparison of two rapture passages, John 14:1-3 and First Thessalonians 4:13-18, shows that a Pre-Tribulation rapture is necessary. Indeed, when we look at the words of Jesus, and compare them with Paul's description of the rapture, we find these passages assume a Pre-Tribulation rapture. John records Jesus saying the following.

> Do not let your hearts be troubled. You believe in God; believe also in me. My Father's house has many rooms; if that were not so, would I have told you that I am going there to prepare a place for you? And if I go and prepare a place for you, I will come back and take you to be with me that you also may be where I am (John 14:1-3).

Jesus says that not all believers will die. One day He will come back for those who are living. However, Jesus must first go back to His Father's house, heaven, to prepare that place for them. When He returns He will bring these believers to His Father's house. This is clear from Jesus' statement "where I am you may also be."

First Thessalonians also gives the same promise to the believers. The Apostle Paul wrote.

> Brothers and sisters, we do not want you to be uninformed about those who sleep in death, so that you do not grieve like the rest, who have no hope. For we believe that Jesus died and rose again, and so we believe that God will bring with Jesus those who have fallen asleep in him. According to the Lord's word, we tell you that we who are still alive, who are left until the coming of the Lord, will certainly not precede those who have fallen asleep. For the Lord himself will come down from heaven, with a loud command, with the voice of the archangel and with the trumpet call of God, and the dead in Christ will rise first. After that, we who are still alive and are left will be caught up together with them in the clouds to meet the Lord in the air. And so we will be with the Lord forever. Therefore encourage one another with these words (1 Thessalonians 4:13-18).

There is also a word of comfort to the believers in each of these passages. Believers are to be comforted by the fact that the Lord will come for His own people and bring them to Himself.

Putting these passages together seems to demand a Pre-Tribulation rapture. Jesus said that the believers would be "where I am." Earlier in John's gospel, the Lord had said the following to the religious leaders who did not believe in Him.

> You will look for me, but you will not find me; and where I am, you cannot come (John 7:34)

Obviously where Jesus was going was not to some place here upon the earth but rather to His Father's house in heaven. However, a Post-Tribulation rapture would have Jesus meeting the believers in the air on His way to earth and then bringing them here, not to His Father's house in heaven. The promise that Jesus made to His disciples, as recorded in John 14, would not come to pass. There must be a time when the raptured believers dwell with Jesus in His Father's house. A

Post-Tribulation rapture does not allow for this but a Pre-Tribulation rapture demands it.

12. THE CHURCH IS PROMISED TO BE REMOVED FROM THE EARTH DURING THE HOUR OF TRIAL (REVELATION 3:10)

There is also the specific promise that the church will be removed from the earth during the "hour of trial." We read the following in the Book of Revelation.

> Since you have kept my command to endure patiently, I will also keep you from the hour of trial that is going to come on the whole world to test the inhabitants of the earth (Revelation 3:10).

This is an explicit promise that the church will not be present during the time of the great tribulation. Jesus promised that believers would be "kept from" this difficult period. This will be accomplished by the catching up of the believers to meet Him in the clouds before the great tribulation occurs.

Notice that they are not said to be "protected during the hour" as some have argued but rather they are "kept from it." This implies removal. In fact, believers are *not* protected during this difficult time. We read in the Book of Revelation about those who were killed during this period.

> When he opened the fifth seal, I saw under the altar the souls of those who had been slain because of the word of God and the testimony they had maintained (Revelation 6:9).

We read that the final Antichrist, described as a beast, is allowed to make war with the saints during the great tribulation. The Bible says.

> It was given power to wage war against God's holy people and to conquer them. And it was given authority over every tribe, people, language and nation (Revelation 13:7)

In response, some say that these believers are protected from God's wrath but not the wrath of the devil. Thus, it is the wrath of Satan that causes their death.

But this doesn't deal with the promise God gives. Whether the wrath comes from God or Satan is not the issue. It's deliverance *from* the time of testing. The wrath, or judgment, comes during this time of testing. God promises to deliver His people from that time.

Thus, this straightforward promise seems to be about as clear as it can be. Those who have trusted Jesus Christ will not have to endure the time of testing, the great tribulation, which will come upon those living on the earth. Instead they will be kept from experiencing it. How? It is through the rapture of the church.

13. THE DAY CANNOT BE BOTH KNOWN AND UNKNOWN

Another line of evidence that the coming of Christ is in two stages has to do with a "known" day the Scripture speaks about as well as an "unknown" day.

Jesus made it clear that *nobody*, including Himself while He was here upon the earth, knew the day and hour of His coming.

> But about that day or hour no one knows, not even the angels in heaven, nor the Son, but only the Father (Matthew 24:36).

Later Jesus repeated this. We read.

> So you also must be ready, because the Son of Man will come at an hour when you do not expect him (Matthew 24:44).

Thus, according to Jesus there is an "unknown" day of His coming.

THERE IS A KNOWN DAY!

Yet, we also read in Scripture of a day which will be known to the people living at that time. In the Book of Daniel it says the final Antichrist will make a seven-year covenant with Israel.

> He will confirm a covenant with many for one 'seven.' In the middle of the 'seven' he will put an end to sacrifice and offering. And at the temple he will set up an abomination that causes desolation, until the end that is decreed is poured out on him (Daniel 9:27)

THE COVENANT BROKEN AFTER THREE AND A HALF YEARS

The final Antichrist will break the agreement after three and one half years. He will desecrate the Holy Temple. This is known as the "abomination of desolation." Once this happens the world will experience a time of unprecedented trouble. Jesus Himself confirmed that this final three and one half year period, the great tribulation or the great distress, begins with the abomination of desolation. He said.

> So when you see the abomination of desolation spoken of by the prophet Daniel, standing in the holy place let the reader understand), then let those who are in Judea flee to the mountains. . . . For then there will be great distress, unequaled from the beginning of the world until now--and never to be equaled again (Matthew 24:15–16, 21).

THE BEAST WILL RULE FOR THREE AND A HALF YEARS

This exact time period is confirmed elsewhere in the New Testament. Indeed, we read of a forty-two month period, or three and one half years, in which the beast, the final Antichrist, will rule.

> The beast was given a mouth to utter proud words and blasphemies and to exercise its authority for forty-two months (Revelation 13:5)

Notice there is a definite point where this begins, a specific duration, and finally a definite time when it will end. Further confirmation of this exact period is found elsewhere in Revelation. It says.

> And the woman fled into the wilderness, where she has a place prepared by God, in which she is to be nourished for 1,260 days (Revelation 12:6)

One thousand two hundred and sixty days is forty-two months or three and one half years.

THERE IS ANOTHER WAY OF STATING IT

Later we are told of a period of times, times and half a time when Israel is protected.

> The woman was given the two wings of a great eagle, so that she might fly to the place prepared for her in the wilderness, where she would be taken care of for a time, times and half a time, out of the serpent's reach (Revelation 12:14).

Time, and times, and half a time is another way of saying "three and one half years."

THE PERIOD ENDS WITH THE RETURN OF THE LORD

The short three and one half year period ends at the return of Jesus Christ!

We read the following in the Book of Revelation.

> But the beast was captured, and with it the false prophet who had performed the signs on its behalf. With these signs he had deluded those who had received the mark of the beast and worshiped its image. The two of them were thrown alive into the fiery lake of burning sulfur (Revelation 19:20).

Thus, Christ will return to the earth on a "known day." It will be three and one half years after the "abomination of desolation." Yet elsewhere Jesus said this His coming was on an "unknown day." The known day and the unknown day must be different days. To sum up, the rapture cannot occur at the same time as the Second Coming.

14. UNBELIEVERS ARE TAKEN FIRST AT THE SECOND COMING OF CHRIST

We also find that at the end of the age, when Jesus Christ comes back to the earth to set up His kingdom, the unbelievers are taken *first*. Jesus gave a parable concerning what will take place at the end of the age. He referred to two types of people; the wheat, who are the believers, and the weeds, who are unbelievers. This is what the Lord Jesus said.

> Let both grow together until the harvest. At that time I will tell the harvesters: First collect the weeds and tie them in bundles to be burned; then gather the wheat and bring it into my barn. . . As the weeds are pulled up and burned in the fire, so it will be at the end of the age. The Son of Man will send out his angels, and they will weed out of his kingdom everything that causes sin and all who do evil. They will throw them into the blazing furnace, where there will be weeping and gnashing of teeth. Then the righteous will shine like the sun in the kingdom of their Father (Matthew 13:30, 40-42)

Notice the order. The *weeds* are separated first. They are then gathered and burned. The wheat is then left to enter into the kingdom.

Elsewhere, Jesus taught that this separation would take place at the time He returns to judge the nations. Matthew records Jesus saying the following.

> When the Son of Man comes in his glory, and all the angels with him, then he will sit on his glorious throne. Before him will be gathered all the nations, and he will separate people

one from another as a shepherd separates the sheep from the goats (Matthew 25:31-32).

This further indicates that the rapture must happen *before* the judgment of the nations since the weeds, the unrighteous, are collected first. At the rapture of the church it is the *believers* who are first separated from the unbelievers as they are caught away to be with the Lord. Again, this provides evidence of two separate comings of Christ.

ONLY THE PRE-TRIBULATION RAPTURE BEST EXPLAINS THE TOTALITY OF EVIDENCE

In conclusion, we stress that it is not simply one verse or one passage which makes Pretribulationism the better answer to the rapture question but rather a combination of various lines of reasoning. True, many of the arguments for Pre-Tribulationism are implications from Scripture. Yet these implications must mean something. If they do not mean what those holding this view claim that they mean then a better explanation must be given. As of now, a better explanation has not been supplied.

Thus, we believe that the Pre-Tribulation view best explains all the available evidence. Compared with all the other positions on the timing of the rapture, it has fewer problems. Therefore, holding this position on the timing of the rapture of the church seems to make the most sense.

SUMMARY TO QUESTION 18
WHAT IS THE PRE-TRIBULATION RAPTURE POSITION?

The rapture of the church is the doctrine that believers will be caught up to meet the Lord in the air at some time before He comes to set up His kingdom. Those who accept the idea of the rapture disagree as to the timing of the event. The pre-tribulation rapture theory teaches that all true believers in Jesus Christ will be caught up to meet the Lord at least seven years before He returns to the earth. Thus, they will escape the Great Tribulation; the entire seven-year period of judgment. This period is also known as the seventieth week of Daniel. Instead of experiencing the various judgments which occur during this dreadful time, they will escape them through the means of the rapture or translation of the church.

There are a number of reasons as to why Bible-believing Christians hold to the pre-tribulation viewpoint. They include the following.

To begin with, the pre-tribulation viewpoint is the result of a consistent literal interpretation of Scripture. If one interprets Bible prophecy literally they will conclude that Jesus Christ comes secretly for believers some seven years before He comes back to earth. It is only when certain prophecies of the future are spiritualized that the pre-tribulation rapture is rejected.

This is consistent with the way prophecy has been fulfilled in the past. At His first coming, Jesus literally fulfilled the predictions written about the coming Messiah. He was born at the predicted place, Bethlehem, in the predicted family, the family of David, and at the predicted time, before the city of Jerusalem and the temple were destroyed. If prophecies of the first coming of Christ were literally fulfilled as written why should we expect it to be different the second time around?

There is also a glaring omission which gives evidence of a pre-tribulation rapture. The church is noticeably absent during the Great Tribulation period as chronicled in the Book of Revelation. While it is mentioned numerous times in the first three chapters, it is not mentioned at all as being on the earth in chapters 4-19 when these great judgments occur. The best explanation for this is that the church is no longer on the earth.

The reason that the church is not highlighted during the Great Tribulation is because focus is now upon the nation of Israel. Indeed, Israel becomes in the spotlight during this period of God's wrath. Since the last seven years are the seventieth week of Daniel, a time where God deals with Israel, it is not surprising to find Israel center-stage and the church non-existent.

Moreover we should emphasize that the church is unnecessary during this time when God's wrath strikes the earth. The universal message of Christ will be proclaimed by 144,000 Jews, the two witnesses, as well as an angel who circles the earth preaching an eternal gospel. The message will be heard by everyone; there is no need for the church.

The idea of two comings of Christ, one for the believers only and a second time as Judge is consistent with what the Bible teaches on the subject. Indeed, when the Scriptures are compared we find that passages speaking of the rapture are speaking of a different event than the passages about the Second Coming. Any similarities are outweighed by the differences.

Indeed, we find that the destinations are different. At the rapture Christ brings the believers with Him unto His Father's house or heaven. At the Second Coming, Jesus leaves His Father's house and comes to the earth.

At the rapture of the church, Christ gathers the believers to Himself. However, at the Second Coming it is the angels who gather the elect. The rapture of the church is a time of reward for believers while the Second Coming is a time for judgment for the unbelieving world.

In passages picturing the Second Coming of Christ, we never find the rapture clearly mentioned. This gives further evidence that we are looking at two different events. Thus, we see the contrasts between the two events are greater than things in common. This indicates that two specific events are in view separated by an interval of time.

An examination of the central passage on the rapture in First Thessalonians chapter four makes it clear the rapture occurs before the tribulation. The fact that the Thessalonians were not concerned about their own future but rather the future of those who had died, shows, among other things, they were not worried about facing the coming wrath. Their only concern is that their dead loved ones would participate in the blessings associated with the rapture.

The blessed hope of the church is looking for the coming of Christ. However, if the pre-tribulation rapture is not true then the church must first look for the antichrist as well as the various judgments found in the Book of Revelation. This does not seem like a "blessed hope."

Scripture makes it clear that the New Testament church is not subject to God's wrath. However, the entire seven-year period of tribulation is a time when the wrath of God comes upon the people of the earth. Thus, it makes sense that the Christians are removed from this time of trouble.

There is another great omission; there are no warnings about what believers should do or how they are to behave during the Great Tribulation. If believers will experience the Great Tribulation then this omission is hard to understand. Warnings are given about such things as false prophets which are to come as well as how to deal with the present tribulations. Why is nothing said about any future tribulation?

There are also a number of events which seemingly must occur between the time of the rapture and the Second Coming of Christ. This includes the judgment seat of Christ and the preparation for the Marriage Supper of the Lamb. Thus, there must be some interval between the two events.

There is also the promise of Jesus to the Church at Philadelphia. In the Book of Revelation it records Jesus saying that these believers will be kept from the hour of trial which will face the entire earth. This hour of trial is understood to mean the Great Tribulation. These believers are promised to be kept from this difficult period. The best way to understand this promise is to assume they will be removed from the earth when this period occurs.

All things considered, it is the pre-tribulation rapture which best explains all the evidence. It gives a consistent understanding of end-time events as well as providing reasonable answers to the various objections. Therefore, this is the view which should be favored.

What Are Some Of The Major Objections To The Pre-Tribulation Rapture Position? How Are They To Be Answered?

We have indicated that we believe the best answer to the question of the timing of the rapture of the church is found in the Pre-Tribulation view; that the true believers in Jesus Christ will escape the final seven year period before Christ returns by being "caught up" to meet the Lord in the air.

However, as can be imagined, not everyone agrees with this assessment. Indeed, there are a number of objections which are brought against this position. If the Pre-Trib view is correct then these objections must have reasonable answers to them. We believe the objections can be answered in a sensible manner. The following are some of the major objections brought up against the Pre-Tribulation view as well as our answers to them.

OBJECTION 1: PRETRIBULATIONISM IS A NEW DOCTRINE

One of the most-often heard arguments is the claim that Pretribulationism is a relatively new doctrine in the history of the church. Indeed, much effort has been expended to demonstrate that the Pre-Tribulation rapture wasn't conceived of until 1812 or thereabouts. Furthermore, it is often linked to the hysterical ravings of a mystic named Margaret McDonald. The fact that nobody came up with this doctrine until the beginning of the nineteenth century is sufficient reason to reject it. Indeed, if the Pre-Trib rapture is taught in Scripture, then why did it take so long for anyone to discover it? It is argued that this objection alone should cause people to reject the Pre-Trib belief.

PRETRIBULATIONAL RESPONSE

Those who hold to the Pre-Tribulational position respond in at least three ways to this charge. They are as follows.

PEOPLE BEFORE 1812 SAW THE RAPTURE AND THE SECOND COMING AS DISTINCT EVENTS

First, there is evidence that certain believers, before 1812, saw the rapture and the Second Coming as two distinct events separated by time. In fact, there are a number of commentators who taught that there was an interval of time between the rapture of the saints and the Second Coming of Christ.

The earliest on record comes from the writings of Ephraim of Nisibis (A.D. 306-373). He is also known as Pseudo-Ephraim. Ephraim was an important theologian in the Eastern or Byzantine Church. One of his sermons, "On the Last Times, the Antichrist and the End of the World," is preserved in four Latin manuscripts. In this sermon we find a reference to the removal of the church from the world before the great tribulation. It says.

All the saints and elect of God are gathered together before the tribulation, which is to come, and are taken to the Lord, in order that they may not see at any time the confusion which overwhelms the world because of our sins.

There is some question as to whether Ephraim actually wrote this or that it was written by someone influenced by him. However, whoever wrote this, whether Ephraim or one of his immediate followers, clearly believed that the elect would *not* experience the wrath of God which would come upon the world. In his sermon Ephraim makes a distinction between the rapture and the Second Coming of Christ as well as saying there will be a three and a half year period from the time the Lord comes for His saints until He returns to the earth.

Another illustration can be given from the writings of the Baptist preacher Morgan Edwards (1722-1795). Edwards wrote about Bible prophecy. In his writings he concluded that there would be a three and a half year period between the rapture and the start of the Millennium.

Consequently, prior to 1812, certain writers understood the Bible to teach an interval of time between the rapture of the church and the Second Coming of Christ. The fact that some of them believed that the interval lasted three and one half years is not relevant. What is relevant is that they did not see the rapture of the church and the Second Coming of Christ taking place at the same time.

THE DOCTRINE WAS NOT DEBATED UNTIL LATE IN THE NINETEENTH CENTURY

Second, even if the Pre-Tribulation rapture theory did not clearly formulate until later in church history this would not settle the issue. Some of the great doctrines of the church such as the Trinity, the Deity of Jesus Christ, and doctrine of justification by faith, took centuries to be fully understood and put into systematic form. These beliefs are surely more important than the timing of the rapture. Consequently, the fact that no systematic doctrine of the rapture has been developed until recently should not surprise us.

Furthermore, systematic theology, or the establishing of Christian doctrine, is usually formed when the church faces a controversy. In the early years, the church had to answer to the question on the nature of Jesus Christ. Was He God, was He human, or was He both? Out of these discussions came the great doctrinal statements of the church. It took the denial of Jesus' Deity to force the church to form doctrinal statements which acknowledged whom He truly is.

Likewise we find the same thing with the doctrine of justification by faith. It was only when this doctrine became a source of controversy in the Reformation period do we have systematic statements about it from believers. Until then, there was no reason to systematize this belief.

In the same manner, until the issue of the Second Coming of Christ and the rapture of the church became a major point of contention, there was relatively little discussion about it. Thus, it was not until the nineteenth century that these issues began to be seriously debated among Bible-believers. From that time, until the present, this issue has been a topic of discussion and debate. Previously it was not.

Thus, the fact that the doctrine of Pretribulationism has continued to develop in detail over the past two hundred years does not prove the doctrine is something new or that it is contrary to the teaching of the New Testament. Indeed, it has developed in a similar manner to that of other major doctrines in the history of the church.

THE REAL ISSUE: WHAT DOES THE BIBLE SAY?

Third, and most important, there is only one real issue in this question as to the timing of the rapture: what does the Bible teach? The issue is not what certain Christians *after* the time of the apostles believed or did not believe about this matter. Church history cannot solve this problem. At best, any contribution which church leaders and theologians can make to this question is only secondary.

Therefore, this objection to the Pre-Tribulation rapture theory is without merit. Again, the question we must answer is this: what does the Bible say about this topic?

OBJECTION 2: WHY SPEND SO MUCH TIME WARNING THE CHURCH OF JUDGMENTS THEY WILL NEVER EXPERIENCE (REVELATION 6-19)

If the church will never experience the judgments of Revelation 6-19, as the Pre-Tribulational rapture position holds, then why does the

Book of Revelation address the church? Why spend so much time and space explaining events they will never see? It makes more sense to understand these chapters as speaking of a time when the church will still be upon the earth.

PRETRIBULATIONAL RESPONSE

The Book of Revelation does a number of things. For one thing it unveils the future. It tells us God's plan for the present earth as well as for the new heavens and new earth. We know what is going to occur because the Bible tells us so.

In addition, the Book of Revelation completes the unveiling of the plan of God to the human race. Paradise lost in the Garden of Eden finds paradise restored in the Book of Revelation. In doing all of this, it gives the church hope for the future.

Thus, God designed this final book of Scripture for various reasons. Believers are to know what is going to occur in the future and thus conduct their lives in light of these coming events. The fact that a number of chapters reveal what will happen when the church is not on the earth is not relevant to the question of the timing of the rapture.

OBJECTION 3: THERE IS ONLY ONE SECOND COMING: PRETRIBULATIONISM HAS TWO COMINGS OF CHRIST AND THREE RESURRECTIONS

One of the complaints against the Pre-Tribulation doctrine is that it multiplies the comings of Christ and the number of resurrections. Indeed, Pre-Tribulationism says there are two comings of Christ; one "secretly" for believers only and one publicly for the entire world. Furthermore, Pre-Tribulationism says that there will be three separate resurrections of the dead. This seems too complicated. The simplest way to understand this matter is to have one coming of Christ and one general resurrection. Indeed the simplest solution is usually the best.

PRETRIBULATIONAL RESPONSE

This objection should not hold any weight. For one thing, every position on the timing of the rapture recognizes that the coming of Jesus Christ will be in two parts. First, there is Jesus coming in the clouds to meet the church and then His coming to the earth as the Judge. At His return Christ will conquer His enemies and set up His kingdom. There is no debating this. However, here is the question which needs answering: are these two events occurring at the same time or is there some interval between the time Christ comes for the church and comes back to the earth?

The simplest answer to this question may not be the right answer. Indeed, using this same logic it could be argued that the Old Testament only speaks of *one* coming of Christ. Obviously that would be the simplest way of looking at the passages which speak of His coming. Yet we know there are two coming of Christ and that the Scripture predicted these two comings.

Consequently, there is nothing impossible, or against Scripture, about the idea that there are two future comings of Christ and three separate resurrections. Everyone admits the rapture is not the same thing as the Second Coming. So we again state the question: is there an interval between the two phases of the coming of Christ? If so, then how long is the interval? This issue must be decided on the evidence alone not on the supposition that we must look for the simplest answer.

OBJECTION 4: CHRISTIANS ARE TO BE ON THE ALERT FOR THE DAY OF THE LORD

Paul wrote to the Thessalonian Christians that they were to be alert for the coming Day of the Lord. He put it this way.

> For you know very well that the day of the Lord will come like a thief in the night. . . . So then, let us not be like others, who are asleep, but let us be awake and sober (1 Thessalonians 5:2,6).

The Thessalonians were told to remain awake so that the Day of the Lord does not overtake them. However, the Pretribulational view says believers will be removed from the earth *before* the Day of the Lord occurs. Why should they have to remain awake for something they would never experience? The fact that they are told to be alert for the coming Day of the Lord seems to indicate they would participate in it.

PRETRIBULATIONAL RESPONSE

The fact that Paul *may* have warned the Thessalonians to remain awake and alert in light of the coming Day of the Lord does not mean they will personally experience this period any more than Peter assumed his readers would experience the end of the Millennium when he told them to live in light of it. We read Peter saying the following.

> The Lord is not slow in keeping his promise, as some under-stand slowness. Instead he is patient with you, not want-ing anyone to perish, but everyone to come to repentance. But the day of the Lord will come like a thief. The heavens will disappear with a roar; the elements will be destroyed by fire, and the earth and everything done in it will be laid bare. Since everything will be destroyed in this way, what kind of people ought you to be? You ought to live holy and godly lives as you look forward to the day of God and speed its coming. That day will bring about the destruction of the heavens by fire, and the elements will melt in the heat. But in keeping with his promise we are looking forward to a new heaven and a new earth, where righteousness dwell (2 Peter 3:9-13).

The context in Peter's letter speaks of a time when the Lord creates a new heaven and new earth. This is at the end of the Millennium; the thousand year reign of Jesus Christ upon the earth. Peter told his read-ers to live in light of *that* coming era. However, it is a time they will never personally experience while living on earth in these bodies.

Thus, the idea behind Paul's encouragement to the Thessalonians is to live in a godly manner in this world with the knowledge that the Lord will one day judge unbelievers. The timing of the rapture is not what he is addressing

In addition, there are those commentators who do not believe this passage in First Thessalonians was a warning for believers about the Day of the Lord. The warning was to be spiritually awake and sober in this age because we never know what trouble may overtake us. It is not connected to what Paul previously said about the Day of the Lord a few verses earlier.

Whatever the case may be, this passage is certainly not a warning for believers to prepare for the problems associated with the Day of the Lord because they will be experiencing this difficult period.

Thus, it would be fair to conclude that there is no evidence in this passage of a Post-Tribulational rapture.

OBJECTION 5: THERE IS NO MENTION OF THE CHURCH IN HEAVEN IN REVELATION 4-18

One of the main arguments Pretribulationists use is the lack of mention of the church upon the earth during the great tribulation period. In Revelation 4-18, where the tribulation is described, we do not find the term "church" used for those believers who are upon the earth.

However, while it is true that the Greek word for church is not specifically mentioned in Revelation 4-18 in describing those living upon the earth, there is no specific mention of the "church" in heaven at that time either! The church is not mentioned at all.

In point of fact, it is not relevant that the Greek word for church is found in the first three chapters of Revelation and then not found again until chapter twenty. In the first three chapters the Greek term for church *ecclesia* is only used of *local* congregations; it is never used of all the believers in Jesus.

Thus, one can rightly say that the term "church" is never used in the Book of Revelation for the entire body of Christ with one exception; in Revelation 22:16 when the plural form of the word is used. Even this usage may only refer to the seven churches mentioned in the Book of Revelation and not to all believers in Jesus Christ.

Thus, the absence of the word in chapters 4-18 should not surprise us because this specific term is not ever used in the Book of Revelation for all Christians. Thus, the argument that the church has been taken up into heaven during this period is not supported by the lack of mention of this term in the chapters describing the great tribulation.

PRETRIBULATIONAL RESPONSE

There are several ways in which those who hold to the Pretribulational rapture position respond to this.

First, it is argued that while the specific word "church" is not used in these chapters the church is pictured as being in heaven in Revelation 4-18 when the great tribulation is taking place upon the earth.

There are twelve references to the twenty-four elders, beginning in Revelation chapter 4. These elders are believed by many to be representative of the church. If so, then we have evidence of the church in heaven during the time the great tribulation occurs upon the earth.

Furthermore, in Revelation 18:20, we have the following statement which seems to give evidence of believers in heaven during the great tribulation.

> Rejoice over her, you heavens! Rejoice, you people of God!
> Rejoice, apostles and prophets! For God has judged her with
> the judgment she imposed on you (Revelation 18:20).

People of God, apostles and prophets, are all a reference to the church. These individuals are seemingly addressed in heaven *before* the return of Christ to the earth. This shows the church is mentioned in heaven in these chapters though not with the specific word "church."

Then there is the matter of certain terms or concepts which are normally associated with the church. When we examine the description of the great tribulation period we find these words and concepts missing from these chapters. Words such as grace, Father, Holy Spirit, mercy, truth, faith, hope, love, peace, believe, comfort and good are all missing. If the church is on the earth during this time then why don't we find these words or concepts ever used in these chapters? There has to be some reason for these omissions. The best answer would seem to be that the church is not on the earth at this time. Thus, it is not necessary to use the words and concepts associated with the church.

ISRAEL IS HIGHLIGHTED IN THESE CHAPTERS

We again stress that while the church is noticeably missing from Revelation 4-18, the nation of Israel is highlighted during this period. Indeed, we find the 144,000 from Israel emphasized in Revelation chapter seven. We are told that they are distinct individuals who become witnesses for the Lord; twelve thousand men from each of the twelve tribes. Israel moves to center-stage at this time.

Indeed, we find that the satanic attacks in the great tribulation period are against Israel as a nation; not the church! It is the "Jews" which are specifically said to be persecuted during this period, never the church. We read in the Book of Revelation.

> A great sign appeared in heaven: a woman clothed with the sun, with the moon under her feet and a crown of twelve stars on her head. She was pregnant and cried out in pain as she was about to give birth (Revelation 12:1-2).

Later it says.

> She gave birth to a son, a male child, who "will rule all the nations with an iron scepter." And her child was snatched up

to God and to his throne. The woman fled into the wilderness to a place prepared for her by God, where she might be taken care of for 1,260 days (Revelation 12:5-6).

The woman gives birth to a male child who will rule the nations. The male child is a reference to Jesus Christ. This same woman then suffers persecution during the great tribulation period. The description of the woman is a description of Israel, not the church. Indeed, Israel brought forth Christ and Christ, in turn, brought forth the New Testament church. The church did *not* bring forth Him.

In fact, during the great tribulation, we are told that the devil himself specifically targets Israel for his attacks. For example, we read of how the serpent, the devil, attempts to destroy the woman after he has been cast out of heaven. Scripture speaks of the following scenario.

> Therefore rejoice, you heavens and you who dwell in them! But woe to the earth and the sea, because the devil has gone down to you! He is filled with fury, because he knows that his time is short. When the dragon saw that he had been hurled to the earth, he pursued the woman who had given birth to the male child. The woman was given the two wings of a great eagle, so that she might fly to the place prepared for her in the wilderness, where she would be taken care of for a time, times and half a time, out of the serpent's reach. Then from his mouth the serpent spewed water like a river, to overtake the woman and sweep her away with the torrent. But the earth helped the woman by opening its mouth and swallowing the river that the dragon had spewed out of his mouth. Then the dragon was enraged at the woman and went off to make war against the rest of her offspring—those who keep God's commands and hold fast their testimony about Jesus (Revelation 12:12-17).

Israel is supernaturally protected by the Lord from the attempted destruction by the devil. Again, we must not miss the fact that the nation *Israel* is targeted.

THE BELIEVING REMNANT

There is also a believing remnant during the period of the great tribulation which is made up of both Jews and Gentiles. They are called the people of God. We read about this in Revelation.

> This calls for patient endurance on the part of the people of God who keep his commands and remain faithful to Jesus (Revelation 14:12).

Later, we see the people of God being urged to come out from among the evil people of the earth. The Bible says.

> Then I heard another voice from heaven say: Come out of her, my people, so that you will not share in her sins, so that you will not receive any of her plagues (Revelation 18:4)

Again, we find *no* specific reference to the church on earth in this entire section dealing with the great tribulation. The people of God are those Jews and Gentiles who have put their faith in Jesus Christ *after* the church has been removed. They, along with the nation of Israel, are the targets of persecution.

Since there is no specific mention of the church in these chapters the logical implication is that the church is no longer upon the earth during this period of judgment.

OBJECTION 6: THE FINAL ANTICHRIST MUST COME FIRST

Another common objection to a Pre-Tribulation rapture concerns Paul's statement that the final Antichrist must arrive *before* the day of the Lord. He wrote.

Concerning the coming of our Lord Jesus Christ and our being gathered to him, we ask you, brothers and sisters, not to become easily unsettled or alarmed by the teaching allegedly from us—whether by a prophecy or by word of mouth or by letter—asserting that the day of the Lord has already come. Don't let anyone deceive you in any way, for [that day will not come] until the rebellion occurs and the man of lawlessness is revealed, the man doomed to destruction (2 Thessalonians 2:1-3).

Until the "man of lawlessness" arrives, who is the final Antichrist, the Lord cannot return. This seems to indicate that the church will see this coming "man of sin."

PRETRIBULATION RESPONSE

Some in Thessalonica were afraid that they may have already entered the great tribulation. To correct this misunderstanding Paul told them the final Antichrist must first be revealed before this intensive time of trouble occurs. In other words, they could not be experiencing this awful period because the man of sin has not yet been revealed.

THE MAN OF SIN IS BEING HELD BACK

The Apostle Paul then states that this coming "man of sin" is being "held back," or restrained, *until* something or someone is removed from the world.

He wrote the following to the Thessalonians.

For the secret power of lawlessness is already at work; but the one who now holds it back will continue to do so till he is taken out of the way. And then the lawless one will be revealed, whom the Lord Jesus will overthrow with the breath of his mouth and destroy by the splendor of his coming (2 Thessalonians 2:7-8).

In fact, this final Antichrist *cannot* be revealed until the restrainer has been taken out of the way. Who or what is restraining Antichrist? The best answer as to the identity of the restrainer is the indwelling Holy Spirit at work through the lives of Christians. Only God Himself has the power to restrain this "man of sin." Once the Christians are removed, through the rapture of the church, then the final Antichrist can be revealed. Consequently, rather than being a passage which contradicts a Pre-Tribulation rapture it actually strongly supports it.

To sum up, before the final Antichrist can arrive on the scene the power which is restraining Him must be removed. This is best understood as the supernatural power of God the Holy Spirit working in the lives of the believers; the New Testament church.

BELIEVERS WILL BE DELIVERED FROM THE WRATH

There is something else. After Paul writes about this judgment of the future man of sin, as well as the judgment of his followers (verses 11-12) he then gives thanks to God for "salvation" or "deliverance." He put it this way.

> But we ought always to thank God for you, brothers and sisters loved by the Lord, because God chose you as firstfruits to be saved through the sanctifying work of the Spirit and through belief in the truth (2 Thessalonians 2:13).

What salvation or deliverance does Paul have in mind? The immediate context would suggest that the salvation Paul is writing about is the same promise of deliverance from the persecution and worldwide judgments that will take place during the Day of the Lord, the rapture.

This is consistent with what Paul had written in his previous letter to the Thessalonians (1 Thessalonians 4:18, 1 Thessalonians 5:9) where he was also addressing the subject of deliverance from the judgments of the Day of the Lord. God made it clear that He has not appointed His people, the Christians, to wrath but rather to deliverance or salvation.

To sum up, this passage in Second Thessalonians gives far more evidence of a Pre-Tribulation rapture than one which would take place after the "man of sin" arrives on the scene.

Objection 7: Why Is The Church Removed From The Time Of Wrath But The 144,000 And Tribulation Saints Are Not?

It is often contended that the church must be removed from the earth before the time of God's wrath because God has not appointed His people to experience His judgment but rather deliverance.

However, everyone admits that during the great tribulation there will be believers upon the earth; the Jewish remnant and the tribulation saints. If God does not remove *them* from this time period then why should He remove the church? Why remove one set of believers but allow another group to suffer His wrath? This seems to take away one of the strongest arguments for the Pre-Tribulation rapture.

RESPONSE

This is a fair question and it can be answered a number of ways. The simple answer to this is that God has made a sovereign decision to keep the Christians, the New Testament church, from His divine wrath. In fact, He has made a number of special promises to them. He has *not* made those same promises to those who become believers during the great tribulation.

We need to keep something in mind. Those who are saved during the great tribulation are recipients of God's amazing grace. Indeed, they had rejected Jesus Christ until the time of the rapture of the church. Yet, God, in His abundant mercy, will still allow them to believe in Christ though they will have to endure this difficult period.

Some of those living during the tribulation period, such as the 144,000 will be protected from His judgments. However, this does not seem to be true for everyone.

Thus, the fact that the church has received special promises from God does not mean that others have the same promise. They do not.

THE OBJECTIONS AGAINST PRE-TRIBULATIONISM ARE ANSWERABLE

This sums up some of the usual objections to the Pre-Tribulation rapture view as well as the responses given to these objections. As can be seen, none of these objections are fatal to the theory. Each objection can be explained in light of what the Pre-Tribulation theory teaches about the events surrounding the catching up of believers to meet the Lord.

While these responses may not persuade everyone that the Pre-Tribulation theory is the best way to understand the question as to the timing of the rapture of the church, it should be noted that these answers are reasonable. Indeed, they do make sense. Whether or not one thinks they make the *best* sense is up to each person to decide.

However, the Pre-Tribulation position does have sensible answers to all the objections brought up against the theory. In contrast, all of the other theories have problems which are seemingly insurmountable.

SUMMARY TO QUESTION 19
WHAT ARE SOME OF THE MAJOR OBJECTIONS TO THE PRE-TRIB RAPTURE POSITION? HOW ARE THEY TO BE ANSWERED?

The belief that the church will be taken out of the world some seven years before the coming of Jesus Christ to the earth, the pre-tribulation rapture, is a doctrine shared by many. However, there have been a number of objections to it. These objections are met with reasoned responses. The objections and responses can be summarized as follows.

Pre-tribulationism is said to be a new belief among Christians. In fact, its history can only be traced as far back as about 1812. Before that time, there was no idea of a pre-tribulation rapture. This being the case, the doctrine should be suspect.

Those who hold the pre-tribulation view do not accept this objection as valid. For one thing, there is evidence that the idea of a rapture occurring before the tribulation was held by some people before the nineteenth century.

Indeed, the writings of fourth century theologian Pseudo-Ephraim demonstrate that he believed an interval of time existed between the rapture of the church and the Second Coming of Christ. Baptist pastor Morgan Edwards, writing in the eighteenth century, also concluded there would be an interval of time between the rapture and the beginning of the millennial reign of Christ. Therefore, this objection has no merit.

Furthermore, the fact that we do not find detailed explanations of the pre-tribulation rapture until recently in the history of the church should not surprise us. For one thing, it takes time for the understanding of doctrines to develop. This is because Christian doctrine is usually put in systematic form only when controversies arise.

For example, the doctrine of the Trinity was clearly formulated in the fourth century when some denied that Jesus Christ is God Himself. The church also had to work through the exact relationship between the human nature and the divine nature of Christ. This occurred at a time when some people were denying either the humanity or deity of Jesus.

The fact is that the church did not face the problem of the timing of the rapture until the end of the 19th century. Before that time there was no real discussion about this issue among Bible-believers. This being the case we should not expect any detailed explanation of the rapture question in the ancient church.

However, this is not really the issue. It does not matter what certain people in church history may or may not have believed about the doctrine of the translation or rapture of the church. The issue is what the Scripture teaches on the matter.

There is also the question as to why the Book of Revelation, a book written for the church, devotes so much space to the Great Tribulation if the church will not be around for these events. This does not seem to make sense. It makes better sense to assume the church is still on the earth during this time and is experiencing the events listed.

This objection is without merit. There are many reasons as to why the Book of Revelation has been composed. For one thing, it completes the revelation of God to the human race. In Genesis, the Lord told us how it all began. In the Book of Revelation, He is telling us how it will all end. In addition, it tells everyone, believer and unbeliever alike, what will occur in the future. The fact that the church may not be around to experience the judgments recorded in chapters six through nineteen is not really relevant to the question of the rapture.

Another objection against pre-tribulationism concerns the coming of Christ and the doctrine of the resurrection of the dead. The pre-tribulation perspective claims there are two comings of Christ and the three resurrections of the dead. However, the Bible only clearly speaks of one coming of Christ and one general resurrection. This seems to put the pre-tribulation view at odds with Scripture.

The response of those holding the pre-tribulation position is as follows. The issue is what the Bible says, not what we may think the Scripture should teach on this issue. We should not pre-determine ahead of time how many times Christ comes or how many times God raises the dead. These are all issues which He decides. Our job is to determine what He has said on the matter. When we look at the Scripture we do find two comings of Christ and at least three times the dead are raised. Thus, there is no problem.

Another objection against Pretribulationism is that the church is not promised to escape suffering; even an unprecedented time of suffering. If the church is to escape such a time there must be clear statements to this effect in Scripture. It is contended that there are not. The ones which hold the pre-tribulation view argue that the Great Tribulation is a unique time which calls for the removal of the church. They believe the unprecedented nature of the period warrants the church not being present.

Furthermore, this period is a time when the Lord once again deals with the nation of Israel. Since Israel will be the main focus of the tribulation period, the church does not have to be present. We never find in Scripture where God is using both Israel and the New Testament church at the same time as His divine agents.

There is the objection that Paul encourages the church at Thessalonica to prepare for the Day of the Lord. Why is this so if they are not going to be around during this period because of the rapture of the church? Why prepare for something they would never experience?

The fact that these believers were told to live in the light of the Day of the Lord should not surprise us. Peter exhorted his readers to live in light of the new heavens and new earth. This would not be realized until the end of the millennium! Thus, the fact that these people were to live in light of future events, even those they would not experience, is really not an issue. Each and every generation of Christians needs to live in light of eternity. Those opposing the pretribulation rapture position note that there is no mention of the church in heaven in Revelation 4-19. Why is this so, if the church is in heaven during this time?

The pre-tribulation response says that there is evidence the church is in heaven during this time of judgment upon the earth. The twenty-four elders, spoken of a dozen times in the Book of Revelation, are worshipping the Lord in heaven. Many believe they are representative of the church.

There is also a reference to saints, apostles, and prophets in heaven during this period. Thus, there is evidence the church is in heaven during this time.

Furthermore, the emphasis during the Great Tribulation period, Revelation 6-19, is on the nation of Israel. Israel once again is highlighted. We find 144,000 men from Israel are supernaturally protected during this period to preach the message of Jesus.

We also discover that the devil specifically targets the nation of Israel for destruction. There is no mention of him targeting the church. The fact that Israel is in the spotlight and the church is not mentioned provides further proof that the church is not present during this Great Tribulation period.

These are the major objections which are usually brought against the pre-tribulation rapture as well as the typical responses to these objections. It is clear that each of these objections has reasonable answers to them. While these answers may not convince everyone, the answers do present a consistent explanation of what will occur in the future with respect to the timing of the rapture of the church.

QUESTION 20

Is There Anything Which Must Take Place Before The Rapture Of The Church Occurs?

This is an often-asked question. Should we expect to see any visible sign before the rapture of the church takes place? Or can the rapture occur at any moment without a sign? What does the Bible say about this topic?

THE PRE-TRIBULATION POSITION: THE RAPTURE IS A SIGNLESS EVENT

If the rapture of the church will happen before the great tribulation, as the Pre-Tribulation rapture position holds, then there are *no* signs before it must occur. Thus, it could happen at any time. The rapture is the next predicted event which will take place before the final count-down to the seven-year period leading up to the Second Coming of Jesus Christ. Nothing *must* occur on the prophetic calendar before the catching up of the church into heaven. In other words, Christ could come for us today!

This is why we must be constantly watching and waiting because none of us knows the exact moment in which it will occur.

ALL OTHER VIEWS: THERE WILL BE MANY SIGNS

Those which do not accept the Pre-Tribulation rapture position believe that there will be signs preceding this event. Indeed, every other theory of the rapture holds that a number of years must pass before the church is caught up to meet the Lord in the air. We can make the following observations.

MID-TRIBULATIONISM: THREE AND ONE HALF YEARS OF SIGNS

The Mid-Tribulation rapture position says the rapture of the church will be at least three and one half years away. Believers must endure the first three and one half years of the final seven-year period, the seventieth week of Daniel. Jesus Christ then comes for His church midway through the last seven year period. Consequently, we should not look for His coming at "any moment."

PRE-WRATH RAPTURE: FIVE AND ONE HALF YEARS OF SIGNS

The Pre-Wrath rapture states that the rapture cannot occur for at least five and one half years. It is not until the seventieth week of Daniel, the final seven years, is three quarters over that the New Testament church, the Christians, will be taken out of the world. Before that time, believers will see a number of end-time events which are predicted in Scripture.

POST-TRIBULATIONISM: SEVEN YEARS OF SIGNS

Finally, the Post-Tribulation view says it will be at least seven years before the Lord Jesus comes for the church. All of the events of this great tribulation period will take place while the church is on the earth.

Consequently, before the Lord returns for the Christians the world must experience the coming of the man of sin, the final Antichrist, and the various dreadful events which will follow his coming. This includes persecution and martyrdom of believers on a huge scale.

These are the events which *must* take place before the church is removed from the earth according to all the main rapture views except the Pre-Tribulation position. Only the Pre-Trib view says the rapture can occur at any time and we strongly believe that this is the view that best fits "all the evidence."

SUMMARY TO QUESTION 20
IS THERE ANYTHING WHICH MUST TAKE PLACE BEFORE THE RAPTURE OF THE CHURCH OCCURS?

The Bible teaches that the rapture of the church will occur at some time in the future. The question comes up as to whether there are any signs we are to look for before this event takes place. Christians are divided on this issue.

Those of us who hold to a pre-tribulation rapture believe that the rapture of the church is a signless event. In other words, no predicted event necessarily needs to take place before it occurs. Thus, it could occur at any time. The blessed hope is that believers could be caught up at "any moment" to meet the Lord. This is what the Scriptures teach with respect to the rapture. Consequently, Christians always need to be ready to meet their Lord!

All of the other theories of the timing of the rapture, mid-tribulation view, pre-wrath, and post-tribulation theory, have some type of interval between the beginning of the Great Tribulation and the rapture of the church. Mid-tribulationism says there will be three and one half years, pre-wrath, at least five and one half years, and post-tribulationism, seven years.

Therefore, a number of things would have to happen before the church, the true believers in Jesus, could be removed from the world. This includes the rise of the man of sin, the antichrist, war on a global scale, and horrific persecution of believers which will lead to untold suffering and death. These theories do not find believers escaping *any* of these horrors.

Thus, there are many signs, or events, which of necessity must take place before Christ returns according to all theories of the timing of the rapture except the pre-tribulation view.

How Should Believers Conduct Their Lives In View Of A Pre-Tribulation Rapture?

We have looked in detail at the subject of the rapture of the church. Many truths were discovered. Thus, we now come to a crucial question, which we have already briefly touched on, "Does it make a practical difference as to what view we hold?" The answer is, "Yes." Indeed, it will make a huge difference if we believe we could meet the Lord at any time as opposed to having to be around for the unprecedented events which are recorded in the Book of Revelation.

THE PRACTICAL BENEFITS OF BELIEVING IN A PRE-TRIBULATION RAPTURE

Those who believe that the Scripture teaches that the rapture will occur before the seventieth week of Daniel, or the last seven years before Jesus Christ returns, assert that there are a number of practical benefits of this perspective. They include the following.

1. WE MUST ALWAYS BE READY

One immediate benefit of believing the Lord can come at any time for the church is the readiness factor. If we believe that Jesus Christ can come for us at any moment, then there is always the need to be ready. Indeed, there will be a certain urgency about things which we do in this life because nobody knows the exact time of the rapture. It could happen today!

This same urgency would not apply if we thought the rapture was three and one half years away, five and one half years away or seven years away. The urgency, from the Pre-Tribulation perspective causes us to live our lives with the idea that today *may* be our last day upon the earth.

In addition, Jesus warned about those who say that the Lord's coming is "delayed." We read Him saying the following.

> But suppose that servant is wicked and says to himself, 'My master is staying away a long time,' and he then begins to beat his fellow servants and to eat and drink with drunkards. The master of that servant will come on a day when he does not expect him and at an hour he is not aware of (Matthew 24:48-50).

Therefore, we always need to be spiritually awake because the Lord may come *at any time* for His church.

2. THERE WILL BE URGENCY IN OUR EVANGELISM

The fact that we believe Jesus Christ could come at any moment also affects the way we evangelize the lost. Knowing the possibility that the true church, the believers in Christ, may not be around tomorrow to tell others about Him causes us to act with an intensity we may not have had if we thought His coming was delayed.

In other words, we will not put off things which we need to do. We will do them because if we delay we may *never* have the chance.

3. THERE WILL BE A ZEAL FOR MISSIONS

If one believes Jesus Christ could come at any moment, this should give believers a tremendous desire to support world missions. Again, there is this urgency about getting the message of Christ to a lost world. Before the judgments of the great tribulation begin, the world needs to know that Jesus Christ has come once and that He is coming again.

4. THERE WILL BE EXCITEMENT AS WE SEE THE STAGE BEING SET FOR CHRIST'S COMING

There is also excitement in the Pre-Tribulation position. As we look at current events and see the way the world is being readied for the Second Coming of Christ we find that the stage is being set for His return to the earth.

If we believe the rapture of the church will take place some seven years *before* Christ returns to the earth in judgment, then the signs of that return, at least seven years from now, make things all the more exciting. Again we repeat, the rapture could happen today! All of these things are natural or logical results of expecting the Lord to come at any moment.

SUMMARY TO QUESTION 21
HOW SHOULD BELIEVERS CONDUCT THEIR LIVES IN VIEW OF A PRE-TRIBULATION RAPTURE?

It does make a difference as to when we think the rapture of the church will occur. Indeed, our view of the events which the Bible says will come upon the earth will make a big difference with how we live. Those who hold the pre-tribulation rapture view contend that there are a number of practical benefits of believing that Christ could return at any moment.

First, we will always have the need to be ready. Indeed, if Christ could return at any time then we should have our lives in order. While this should be the case whether or not we believe the Lord could return at any time, because we don't know how long we will have on the earth, there is a special urgency about how we conduct our lives. There will also be a real urgency about our personal evangelism of the lost. If we believe our time may be short, then we will redouble our efforts to preach the gospel to these people whom the Lord has placed in our lives. Since we cannot be certain we will be around tomorrow to reach these people, we will make an effort to reach them today.

World missions will get a boost from believers if we suppose Christ could come for His church at any moment. The lost people of this world need to hear about Jesus' claims from those who know Him. However, once the believers are taken up to meet the Lord in the air there will be a time when they will not personally hear from those who have trusted Christ.

Indeed, though there will be people who become believers in the Great Tribulation period, there will not be anyone who has developed spiritual maturity through years of knowing the Lord. All believers during that time will be new believers. Yet before the rapture happens, people can hear firsthand from those who have a lifetime of personal experiences with the Lord. This will not be true after the rapture takes place.

The pre-tribulation view also lends itself to excitement about the days in which we live. Current events are understood in the light of what Scripture predicts is to come. While some people may read too much into current happenings this should not cause us to ignore what is going on. If the stage is being set regarding the Second Coming of Christ, then the rapture, which occurs some seven years before, may not be far off. Indeed, He may be coming for us today!

QUESTION 22

Can Anyone Know The Exact Date
When The Rapture Will Take Place?
(Date-Setting)

The rapture of the church is a coming event. At some time in the future, the Lord Jesus will descend from heaven and gather all who have believed in Him, the living and the dead, unto Himself. This is something which Christians are looking forward to occur. Indeed, it is our "blessed hope."

This being the case, the question arises as to the possibility of knowing *when* this will occur. Is there any indication in Scripture that humans can know the *exact* date and time of the rapture of the church? Has God revealed that information?

A number of points are necessary to understand when answering this important question. They include the following.

1. WE CANNOT KNOW THE ANSWER AS TO WHEN JESUS WILL RETURN FOR BELIEVERS

The Bible is clear that nobody on the earth can know the answer to this particular question. This comes from the words of Jesus as well as those of the Apostle Paul.

JESUS SAID WE CANNOT KNOW

Jesus made it clear that the timing of His return for the believers has not been revealed to the human race. The Lord urged us to be ready because we do not know the time He will come. Matthew records Jesus saying the following.

> Therefore keep watch, because you do not know on what day your Lord will come (Matthew 24:42)

Elsewhere Jesus said His coming will be at a time when people are not expecting it. Again, we read Matthew recording Jesus saying.

> So you also must be ready, because the Son of Man will come at an hour when you do not expect him (Matthew 24:44).

In another place, Jesus specifically says that we do not know the day or the hour of His return. Matthew records Him saying.

> Therefore keep watch, because you do not know the day or the hour (Matthew 25:13)

After His resurrection from the dead Jesus again emphasized these things are not ours to know. We read the following in the Book of Acts.

> Then they gathered around him and asked him, "Lord, are you at this time going to restore the kingdom to Israel?" He said to them: "It is not for you to know the times or dates the Father has set by his own authority. But you will receive power when the Holy Spirit comes on you; and you will be my witnesses in Jerusalem, and in all Judea and Samaria, and to the ends of the earth" (Acts 1:6-8)

These passages which record the words of Jesus should make it clear that such knowledge about the timing of the Lord's coming for the believers "in Christ" has not been given to us.

PAUL SAID WE CANNOT KNOW

The Apostle Paul also emphasized that we cannot know the day or the hour when the Lord comes for the church. He said.

Now, brothers and sisters, about times and dates we do not need to write to you, for you know very well that the day of the Lord will come like a thief in the night (1 Thessalonians 5:1,2).

Therefore, we have the New Testament consistently teaching that the exact time of the Lord's coming is not something which God has allowed us to know.

2. JESUS HIMSELF DID NOT KNOW THE ANSWER TO THIS QUESTION WHILE HERE ON EARTH

It should be obvious that we cannot know the time the Lord will return for His church. Indeed, we are told that Jesus said He didn't know the exact time He would come back! Matthew records Jesus saying the following about His coming.

But about that day or hour no one knows, not even the angels in heaven, nor the Son, but only the Father (Matthew 24:36).

Jesus said the day and hour was known by God the Father alone. If while on earth, the God-man, Jesus Christ, did not know the day or the hour of His return, then there is no reason to suppose that we can know what He did not know.

3. HAS GOD TOLD US THE ANSWER SINCE THE TIME JESUS ASCENDED INTO HEAVEN?

Some may argue that God has revealed truths to us about the timing of Jesus' return after He ascended into heaven. Therefore, we can know the exact time when He will return and take the believers to be with Him in "His Father's house." In other words, once Jesus left the earth and returned to heaven, God then revealed enough information so we can set certain dates.

To support this idea, there is a passage in the Book of Daniel which speaks of the increase of knowledge in the "last days. We read the following.

> But you, Daniel, roll up and seal the words of the scroll until the time of the end. Many will go here and there to increase knowledge (Daniel 12:4)

In the last days knowledge shall increase. This has to do with knowledge of how to interpret the Book of Daniel. The Book of Daniel will more fully be understood at the time of the end. That time is now.

Thus, while the early church did not know the day or hour of His coming, those living in the last times will be able to calculate it because of our increase in knowledge of the Book of Daniel.

There is also a statement of Jesus which is used to support this idea. Luke records Him saying the following.

> When these things begin to take place, stand up and lift up your heads, because your redemption is drawing near (Luke 21:28).

Again, this could be understood to mean those living at the last times will know when the end is about to occur.

RESPONSE

While it is true that the Lord has given us further understanding with respect to the coming again of Christ there is nothing that specifically tells us *when* this will occur. We do have more information to correctly interpret prophetic matters. However, this does not mean that the day and the hour of the rapture of the church have been revealed to us. They have not.

In addition, we should note that Jesus' statement commanded the believers to watch. However, they were never told to set dates for His coming!

Thus, if Jesus did not know the time of His return and God hasn't revealed the exact date and time of the rapture of the church since Jesus was on the earth, then we *cannot* know.

4. WE CANNOT KNOW SO WE SHOULD NOT SPECULATE

This brings us to our last point which cannot be overemphasized. Since we cannot know the exact time the rapture of the church will take place there is *no* room for speculation.

Unhappily history affords us with a number of examples of people who believed they knew the precise time of the Lord's return to the earth. Whether it be through some special revelation they thought they received, or from some calculations made from Scripture, they publicly stated what they believed would be the time of the coming of Christ for His own.

Obviously all of them have been wrong. Accordingly, from Scripture we can conclude that we cannot know when Jesus Christ will return for His church.

Furthermore, we should not speculate about the timing of this event. Anyone who claims to know or engages in speculation is acting contrary to the direct teachings of the Bible; no matter how sincere the motives may be.

SUMMARY TO QUESTION 22
CAN ANYONE KNOW THE EXACT DATE WHEN THE RAPTURE WILL TAKE PLACE? (DATE-SETTING)

One of the things which every believer would like to know would be the exact time the rapture of the church takes place. Can we know? Is it possible to discover the exact day and hour of the Lord's return for His church at the rapture?

The Bible says it is not possible to know. Scripture gives no indication that humans can have the answer to this question.

Jesus made it clear that nobody knows the time of His coming. In fact, He did not even know when this would occur while He was here upon the earth!

Some argue that since the time Jesus was on the earth God has subsequently revealed this truth to His people. Now that the Scriptures are complete there is enough information to calculate the time. Furthermore, we have a specific statement in the Book of Daniel which says that this book will be understood by those at the time of the end. Since we are now at the time of the end we should be able to calculate these truths which were hidden from believers of an earlier time.

However, this is not the case. While we do have much more knowledge to be able to correctly interpret coming prophetic events this does not include the day and hour when Christ will return for His church. That particular prophetic truth has not been revealed to us.

Given these above facts, we should not ever attempt to speculate as to when we think the Lord will return. Indeed, since Scripture says we do not know the answer to this question, and that we cannot know the answer, we should not engage in wild speculation about something which God has not revealed.

Those who have claimed to know the date and time of Christ's coming in the past, whether from some special revelation they have claimed to receive, or from some calculations they have made from Scripture because of increase of prophetic knowledge, have all be wrong in their claims.

Therefore, what we can know for certain is that when someone claims to have knowledge of the timing of the rapture of the church they are wrong in their claims and they are contradicting what Scripture itself says about this issue. Consequently we should *never* take their c laims seriously.

What Will Happen To Babies, Young Children, And The Mentally Challenged When The Rapture Occurs?

When the rapture of the church transpires all those who have believed in Jesus Christ will be caught up to meet Him in the clouds. The dead in Christ will be raised first and then the living believers will join them. There is no doubt about this.

However, there is some question as to what will happen to babies and younger children. What will be their fate when the rapture takes place? Also, there is also the question about those whose mental capacity has not progressed past that of an infant or a young child. Thus, when we answer the question as to the destiny of children we will also be referring to those whose mental ability did not develop beyond that of a child.

Will they be taken with the believing adults or will they be left behind? Does the Bible make a distinction between what will occur with the children of believers as opposed to the children of unbelievers? What does the Scripture have to say about this?

Christians have come up with the following options.

OPTION 1: IT IS A NON-ISSUE WITH A POST-TRIB RAPTURE

If the rapture of the church happens at the end of the great tribulation, when Jesus Christ is returning to the earth, then this is really a non-issue. Christ returns at the same time as the rapture. He destroys His enemies and then judges those who remain. There is no significant interval of time when believing parents who are raptured could possibly be separated from their children.

However, if there is an interval of time between the rapture and the Second Coming then the remaining options are as follows.

OPTION 2: ALL CHILDREN WILL BE TAKEN IN THE RAPTURE

There are those who think that *all* children will be gathered up with the living believers when they meet the Lord in the air. Many people hold to this position. They assume that when babies and young children die they will automatically go to meet the Lord. Since this is the case, the Lord would not allow babies and younger children to suffer the unprecedented horrors of the great tribulation.

However, these are two different issues. One has to do with the eternal destiny of those who die in infancy while the other has to do with babies and children living through a difficult period of time upon the earth.

Furthermore, there is no indication in Scripture that this is what will happen to all children.

OPTION 3: NO CHILDREN WILL BE TAKEN IN THE RAPTURE

Others take the opposite approach. They feel that *no* children will be taken in the rapture because this event is limited to those who have personally believed in Jesus Christ. By definition, babies and small children are not able to do this.

We have a number of biblical precedents for this. At the flood of Noah the children of the wicked were left to perish in the flood; they were not spared the judgment because of their age. At the city of Sodom only Lot, his wife, and daughters were spared the judgment. None of the children of the wicked sodomites were spared.

When Israel destroyed the cities of Canaan, God commanded them to kill everyone. Again, nobody was spared from this judgment of the Lord.

However there is a huge problem with this position. The unbelieving parents would still be around to take care of *their* children but there would be nobody to take care of the children of believers if all children were left behind. A better answer needs to be found.

OPTION 4: ONLY CHILDREN OF BELIEVERS WILL BE TAKEN IN THE RAPTURE

A better idea says that only the children of believers will be gathered to meet the Lord at the rapture of the church. Indeed, it would be a very cruel thing to leave them behind to experience the horrors of the great tribulation as their Christian parents are being raptured.

In addition, it would seem like a penalty for those Christians which were taken. They enter the joy of the Lord but their innocent children would be left to suffer, unattended, the judgments of the great tribulation. It is hard to imagine that this will happen.

Consequently, it is assumed that children of believers will be caught away with their believing parents in the rapture of the church.

Furthermore, there seems to be biblical evidence that this is what will occur. Paul wrote that the children of believers are sanctified, or set apart, for the Lord.

> For the unbelieving husband has been sanctified through his wife, and the unbelieving wife has been sanctified through her believing husband. Otherwise your children would be unclean, but as it is, they are holy (1 Corinthians 7:14).

In some sense, the believers in the family, "sanctify" or set apart the other family members who are not believers. In this passage we note that the children are specifically said to be "holy" because of a believing family member.

To many, this indicates that children of believers will be included with the adults when the rapture occurs.

This appears to be the best way to understand the answer to this question as to the fate of children at the rapture. The children of believers will be taken up to meet the Lord but there is no such assurance for the children of unbelievers.

SUMMARY TO QUESTION 23
WHAT WILL HAPPEN TO BABIES AND YOUNG CHILDREN WHEN THE RAPTURE OCCURS?

The rapture of the church will take all true believers from the world. Scripture clearly teaches this. Unbelievers will be left behind. But what will be the destiny of the babies, young children and the mentally challenged? Will they also be left behind? What does the Bible say?

The answer to this question is simple: the Bible does not say. We do not know what will happen to infants and small children when the rapture occurs because Scripture does not give us any information. This has led people to speculate as to what may happen to them, but we must remember that this is purely speculation on anyone's part.

If the rapture occurs at the time of the Second Coming of Christ, then this is a non-issue. Hence, we do not have to concern ourselves about children possibly living through the worst time of trouble that planet earth ever will experience. Christ would immediately set up His kingdom and judge the wicked. The children would not have to suffer the judgment of the great tribulation without their parents to look after them.

If there is an interval between the time of the rapture and the Second Coming then this does become an issue. There are a number of possible scenarios.

Some feel that all children will be caught up to meet the Lord. By virtue of the fact that they have not reached an age of accountability they will be removed to the earth so they do not have to experience the horrors of the great tribulation.

Others take the opposite approach. They believe that no children will be taken in the rapture of the church. Since the translation of the church is the catching up of believers babies and very young children would not qualify.

There is another approach which is a compromise between these two. It says that only children of believers will be raptured. Scripture says the believing parents set apart or sanctify their children. This is understood to mean that these particular children will be taken. In addition, there are a number of biblical accounts where children were not spared because of the sins of their parents. This would explain why children of unbelievers are not taken.

To sum up, we are not told the answer to this question. This being the case we should leave the fate of these children in the hands of an all-knowing, all-loving God who has decided not to tell us what He is going to do in this matter.

QUESTION 24

What Final Observations And Conclusions Should We Make About The Subject Of The Rapture?

We have attempted to touch upon the major issues with respect to the rapture of the church. As we have seen, it is a topic in which good Bible-believing Christians have come to different conclusions. There is no agreement as to the purpose of the rapture, the timing of the rapture, or who will be raptured. However, for a number of reasons, we have concluded that the Pre-Tribulation position best fits all the biblical facts.

After looking at these issues from the various perspectives there are several observations and conclusions that we should make. They are as follows.

1. WE SHOULD NOT IGNORE THIS TOPIC

One thing which does stand out as we survey the issue of the rapture of the church is that we should not ignore this important topic. While the timing of the rapture is not the same as the gospel of Jesus Christ, our understanding of it has ramifications on how we will conduct our lives. Indeed, it will make a difference on how we go about our daily living as well as how we prepare for the future.

If we believe that Christians will experience the horrors of the great tribulation period and the persecution and martyrdom surrounding it, then we will make the necessary preparations. If we are alive when this period takes place then we must be ready for what will occur.

However, if we come to the conviction that the New Testament church, the Christians, will escape this period through the rapture we will live in accordance with that belief since we have a different view of our future.

Instead of looking for the judgments of the great tribulation we are looking for the "any moment" coming of Christ for the church.

2. SOME PEOPLE MAY NOT COME TO ANY FIRM CONCLUSIONS

After examining all the views with respect to the timing of the rapture, some people may not come away with any firm convictions as to when it will occur; they may not feel comfortable embracing any particular view at this time. There is certainly nothing wrong with this. Indeed some individuals may need more time to work through and reflect upon these issues before reaching a conclusion in their own mind.

3. IT IS POSSIBLE TO KNOW CERTAIN THINGS

However, we also find that it is possible to know a number of things about the rapture of the church. While the timing may be disputed, other things about this event are plain for all to see. We know that Christ will return for believers and that once He takes us to Himself we shall forever be with Him. This is the blessed hope which all Christians have.

4. WE SHOULD UNIFY ON THE THINGS WE ALL AGREE

This last point cannot be overemphasized. Until the time the Lord comes back there will be disagreements among Bible-believers as to this issue. This is a fact. However, we should not let this lack of agreement cloud more important issues; the things we do agree upon.

All Bible-believers are looking forward to the time when Jesus Christ returns, when He gives new bodies to believers, judges the living and the dead, and then sets up His everlasting kingdom. All of us, no matter what our position on the rapture of the church, have this hope. It is these areas which we should emphasize among ourselves; not the things we disagree upon.

While it is certainly appropriate to discuss and debate the prophetic details contained in Scripture we should never lose sight of the greater issues.

We are one body in Jesus Christ and we should act as one. The greater goal of preaching the message of Christ to the world should always be foremost in our minds. We should never take our eyes off of this goal.

The Apostle Paul stated it in this manner.

> Make every effort to keep the unity of the Spirit through the bond of peace (Ephesians 4:3).

We could not agree more!

SUMMARY TO QUESTION 24
WHAT FINAL OBSERVATIONS AND CONCLUSIONS SHOULD WE MAKE ABOUT THE SUBJECT OF THE RAPTURE?

We have examined a number of issues with respect to the doctrine of the rapture, or the translation, of the church. After looking at this matter in some detail there are a number of observations and conclusions which we can make. They can be summed up as follows.

To begin with, we realize that the rapture of the church is a significant doctrine though not the most important doctrine in Scripture. It does have ramifications as to how we will conduct our lives. For example, if we believe the church will experience the Great Tribulation period, then we will prepare our lives differently than if we believe the church will escape this period. Thus, we should not ignore this topic because it does have practical implications. Furthermore, we should not ignore it because it is taught in Scripture and all Scripture must be studied.

As we have emphasized, each rapture position has its particular problems and questions which it must answer. Therefore, there is the possibility that some people may not come to any firm conclusions on this topic. After examining all of the evidence they may not feel comfortable with any of the stated positions. They will place this issue into the category of "undecided." There is nothing wrong with coming to this position if a person truly cannot make up his or her mind. However, we again stress that it is possible to know certain things about this glorious coming event. Even if we cannot agree on the timing of it, we can rejoice in the great truth that someday the living believers will be taken up to meet the Lord in the air and forever be with Him. This is something which all true believers can agree upon. In sum, believers "in Christ" should unify around what we do know to be true and hold our views with grace and humility on those issues where brothers and sisters are divided.

A Look At Some Contrasts Between The Rapture Of The Church And The Second Coming Of Christ

The main passages for the rapture of the church are John 14:1-3, 1 Thessalonians 4:13-18 and 1 Corinthians 15:51-58. The main passages for the Second Coming of Christ include Zechariah 14:1-21, Matthew 24:29-31, and Revelation 19. When we compare these passages we find the following contrasts and differences.

RAPTURE: JESUS COMES FOR THE BELIEVERS SECOND COMING: HE RETURNS WITH THE BELIEVERS

At the rapture Jesus comes for His own (John 14:1-3, 1 Thessalonians 4:13-18). However, at the Second Coming, Jesus comes *with* His own (Revelation 19)

Rapture: Jesus Meets Believers In The Air Second Coming: He Comes To The Earth With The Believers

At the rapture Jesus meets believers in the air (1 Thessalonians 4:17) while at His Second Coming He comes to the earth (Zechariah 14:4, Revelation 1:7, Acts 1:10-12)

RAPTURE: JESUS CLAIMS HIS BRIDE SECOND COMING: JESUS RETURNS WITH HIS BRIDE

At the rapture Jesus claims His bride (1 Thessalonians 4:13-18) while at the Second Coming Jesus returns with His bride (Revelation 19).

RAPTURE: ONLY BELIEVERS SEE HIM SECOND COMING: EVERYONE SEES HIM

Only believers will see Him at the rapture (1 Thessalonians 4:13). However, at the Second Coming every eye will see Him (Revelation 1:7).

RAPTURE: NO SIGNS SECOND COMING: SIGNS PRIOR

No signs precede the rapture while there are signs which occur prior to the Second Coming (Matthew 24:4-28, Revelation 19:11-21).

RAPTURE: THE DATE IS UNKNOWN SECOND COMING: THE DATE WILL BE KNOWN

The rapture could happen at any moment (1 Thessalonians 5:2,6). Yet the Second Coming will be at a known date for those living at that time (Daniel 9:27,12:11).

RAPTURE PASSAGES: NO REFERENCE TO SECOND COMING SECOND COMING PASSAGES: NO CLEAR REFERENCE TO RAPTURE

Interestingly, when we look at the rapture passages there is nothing specifically said about the Second Coming in those particular contexts. Likewise, in the Second Coming passages there is no indisputable reference to the rapture.

RAPTURE: ALWAYS CONTEXT OF BLESSING SECOND COMING: ALWAYS A CONTEXT OF JUDGMENT

In the rapture passages the emphasis is on the blessings that the believers will receive. However, the Second Coming passages are set in a context of tribulation, wrath, and judgment.

RAPTURE: RESURRECTION OF CHURCH SAINTS SECOND COMING: NO RESURRECTION OF CHURCH SAINTS

The passages on the rapture speak of the resurrection of those who have died in Christ (1 Thessalonians 4:13-18, 1 Corinthians 15:51-58).

However, no passage about the Second Coming mentions anything about the resurrection of church saints.

These contrasts make it clear that we are dealing with two distinct events. The evidence also seems to demand that an interval of time must take place between the rapture of the church and the Second Coming of Jesus Christ.

About the Author

Don Stewart is a graduate of Biola University and Talbot Theological Seminary (with the highest honors).

Don is a best-selling and award-winning author having authored, or co-authored, over seventy books. This includes the best-selling *Answers to Tough Questions*, with Josh McDowell, as well as the award-winning book *Family Handbook of Christian Knowledge: The Bible*. His various writings have been translated into over thirty different languages and have sold over a million copies.

Don has traveled around the world proclaiming and defending the historic Christian faith. He has also taught both Hebrew and Greek at the undergraduate level and Greek at the graduate level.

57344292R00135

Made in the USA
San Bernardino, CA
20 November 2017